Would it kill you to put on some lipstick?

1 YEAR AND 100 DATES

Would it kill you to put on some lipstick?

1 YEAR AND 100 DATES

HOLLY MARTYN

A MEMOIR/MANUAL

Glitterati Editions
NEW YORK

For my daughter, with love.

First published in 2020 by

Glitterati Editions

311 West 43 Street
Floor 12
New York, NY 10036
Telephone: 646-584-6382

www.GlitteratiEditions.com
media@GlitteratiEditions.com for inquiries

First edition, 2020

Library of Congress Cataloging-in-Publication data
is available from the publisher.

Hardcover edition ISBN: 978-1-943876-13-6

Printed and bound in China
10 9 8 7 6 5 4 3 2 1

www.hollymartyn.com
Instagram and Twitter: @hollylmartyn

“Everyone needs work on love.”

—my daughter, age 9

Author's Note

This is a work of nonfiction and is the mostly true story of what happened when I decided to stop feeling sorry for myself and rebuild my life following my second divorce. When I decided to take an active role in my social life and test the idea that, in a hundred dates or less, I might actually meet someone special. Some details have been altered in the interest of privacy, such as names and professions, but the spirit of my story remains.

This book can be read as both a memoir and dating manual. I share lessons I learned about getting back out there in midlife, at a time when my confidence was low. If my adventures (and misadventures!) help you in any way, I'll be thrilled.

—HLM

Contents

CHAPTER 1

Let Go or Be Dragged

I've been dumped. Zach, my motorcycle-riding Jesus doppelganger boyfriend of a year and a half decides I'm worth a two-minute phone call and now we're officially done. "I'm done looking" was what he used to say when it came to me, the words his grandfather spoke right before he proposed to his grandmother.

Not that I wanted a proposal. I already have two failed marriages. I just want a partner and dare I say it—love. I still believe in *love*. And by *love,* I mean that feeling of emotional, maybe even spiritual connection, combined with an intellectual and physical bond with another human being. Your person. They're easy to be with, it just works, they're your confidant, partner-in-crime, you two against the world, the one you laugh and share the private jokes with, the person whose inner and outer being feels like home. You love their body,—it's like a part of your own, their smells, the skin-on-skin, the falling asleep and waking up together. You crave them; it's primal. Where there's the element of the irrational and you don't quite know why, but you're just smitten with this person. How you can be in the kitchen making yourself a cup of coffee and look over at them sitting there, simply being, reading a newspaper or something, and their very existence warms you to your core. It's not the person you can live with, it's the person you cannot live without. And then what happens if you lose them?

During highly stressful times in general, and in the love life particularly, we women have a number of options in the pity party tool kit: dramatic haircuts and/or dye jobs; crying alone; crying with girlfriends and/or gay best friends; binge eating and/or heavy drinking (preferably with sickly sweet fruit- flavored vodkas and liquors, or the hard stuff in deep amber); the list goes on. I choose a trip to the spa, as I often do, which is only one white wall and waves-crashing-on-the-shore-soundtrack short of a mental hospital, let's face it.

Slumped by the fireplace in the Relaxation Room in my bathrobe, hairy legs protruding—no one is ever going to see my pudgy, single-mother legs again, so why shave them? *(My boyfriend doesn't want me.)*—drinking my tea and un-gumming the dried apricot off the roof of my mouth *(where the hell is the chocolate, anyway?)*, I reach for a women's magazine.

It falls open to an article written by a journalist who searches most of her twenties and thirties for The One. She finally finds him and marries this absolute love of her life and they have a baby. And just as they are ready to enjoy this new child and a lifetime together, the writer's husband is stricken by cancer and dies.

She is utterly heartbroken. Gutted. Consumed by the life she's lost and the baby she now has to raise alone, she gives herself some time to grieve and, after awhile, in her work as a journalist, she crosses paths with the late comedienne, Joan Rivers. Rivers knows the writer well enough to say: "Would it kill you to put on some lipstick?"

Rivers tells her to get an online dating account, go on one hundred dates, and she'll meet somebody.

There you go, I think, sinking deeper in my chair, staring into the dancing flames of the fireplace, the magazine folding against my bathrobe. *One hundred dates. Problem solved.*

♥

I'm the granddaughter of a former nun who kicked her habit, as our family joke goes. Her daughter, my mother, is a former Catholic-turned-Mormon, now converted Jew, who claims to have conceived my brother, Brent, without having sex.

The tale of the near-immaculate conception was a conversation that my mother chose to have with my younger sister, Margot, but not me. Because I was safe. Perfectly safe, in my mother's estimation, of ever falling accidentally pregnant. At the age of fifteen, I was nearly six feet with Chewbacca-like frizzy blonde hair and the hunchback posture of a tall girl humiliated by her height. I spent my spare time reading or loudly arguing on the debate team. So it was a low probability that any boys were going to be getting into my white cotton briefs anytime soon. I was indeed a virgin.

My sister, on the other hand, was a real problem. As a more petite and graceful long-haired brunette with enormous green eyes, who looks like a cross between Brooke Shields and Sophia Loren, the phone was ringing off the hook, and the boys were pounding down the door of our modest split-level on the outskirts of Vancouver. Margot was taking modeling lessons after school and secretly learning to binge and purge after the agency told her she needed to drop a few pounds. Modeling lessons for me were never discussed. ("But Holly, you walk funny," my mother said on more than one occasion.)

One night when Margot was about fourteen, a boy called on our family's sole black rotary-dial phone and after she'd hung up, my mother lost it. It seemed, at least to my mother, that this particular phone call was the alarm bell sounding on my sister's future. Slumped on the end of Margot's single bed in the basement bedroom, which was plastered with AC/DC, Def Leppard, and Ozzy Osbourne posters, my mother tearfully said that she feared the same fate that befell her would also befall Margot.

"I was a single mother, I was just so lonely. I know that it's against God's law to have premarital sex, so I didn't."

"Wait—but—" Margot said. "I mean, you had to have . . . you know . . .?"

"Oh no, I never let Gary have sexual intercourse with me. That would be wrong." Gary was the man my mother dated at the time and they'd eventually marry, making Gary our stepfather.

"I don't get it," Margot said.

"Heavy petting!" my mother shrieked. I'm guessing she clutched her Adam's apple the way she does when she's vexed, before dissolving in to sobs.

"Huh?"

"He ejaculated outside of me and the sperm swam in!" my mother whispered.

"That happens?"

"Margot! You must be so careful! You cannot have sex outside of marriage!"

"Mom, I'm not having sex," Margot insisted. (Actually, she was, with her boyfriend's father who was driving her to those modeling lessons, but that's another story.)

"I just couldn't have an abortion," my mother continued. "I had to marry Gary."

About a decade later, after my brother, Brent, came out to my mother as gay, she would tell him that she wished she'd had that abortion.

I was in my late teens before Margot warned me of the Perils of Heavy Petting. "Brent was a rim shot!" Margot said. I stared at her with my jaw dropped and then we began laughing hysterically. Rim shot. Every now and then since, Margot likes to coolly work in the term at occasions that require propriety, just to see if I can keep it together.

Brent, bless him, is now an Australian citizen and high school teacher living in Tasmania. I kid you not.

Needless to say, there wasn't a lot of warmth and openness when I was growing up, not to mention candor when it came to sex, boys, dating, or love. It was all wrapped up in pain, religion, dogma, shame, and conniving sperm. I was on my own to figure out the whole messy business. There was a steep learning curve for this awkward girl.

♥

When I began writing this book, Joan Rivers was alive and George Clooney was still a bachelor.

Sadly, Joan has since passed away and George is now married and a father. Life keeps moving, and I suppose the saying is true: nothing endures but change. We have little choice but to adapt to whatever life hands us. And I know more than ever that, when it comes to life, change, and people, we can never change another—we can only work to change and improve ourselves.

If you're currently experiencing your own spa moment, i.e., you're hopeless and unwaxed, I completely get it: you're devastated, if you're anything like me going through my breakups and divorces. You believed in love, marriage, partnership, and family and you stood up publicly in front of anyone who's ever meant anything to you and made vows. You believed and it meant everything. You didn't do anything wrong to want all of that, and you had the courage to try to grab it.

You wanted a good marriage, maybe even an excellent one. It probably took you a long time to meet your significant other, and now you're mourning the loss of those years of building a life together, your incredible investment of self, sacrifice, time. My first marriage failed after a mostly happy decade together when my husband began drinking heavily, had an affair, was diagnosed with bipolar disorder, and refused to take his medication regularly. We were right at the point of starting a family, but I knew that this was not the relationship to bring children into. We were fragile. We divorced, and I then (stupidly) quickly rebounded into my second marriage. I married the first man I dated after my divorce, and they even had the first same name. It was a whirlwind twelve-month courtship and before we knew it, David #2 and I were parents of a beautiful baby girl, Evie. Soon we discovered how incompatible we actually were. Many of the things we'd enjoyed together while dating, like traveling and socializing together, he didn't want to do anymore. He preferred to stay home and follow rigid routines. Eventually, he told me that if we were invited to social events, I should go alone. It felt like I was single again, yet I was married. Still, I wanted another child. Before marriage, we'd agreed that we'd have at least two children, but then he changed his mind. Evie was enough for him and maybe even too much sometimes. In my second divorce, I lost the dream of one happy family living together under one roof, something I'd never had as child. I wanted so much more for my daughter. I'd dug myself deeper. Even my do-over had failed.

Bereft, it brought me to asking myself many questions. *Is it men or is it me?*

That's one. I also realized that one of my biggest mistakes is that I never really dated much when I was younger. I spent my twenties with one David and my thirties with another. Then I became a mother. I had never taken the time to date, explore, and try to figure out who might be the best partner for me. There are so many people out there, so many different personality types, so many possibilities. I began to admit to myself that one of the reasons I'd remarried so quickly was that I was terrified to be alone. I was also afraid to miss out on the opportunity to have a family. Nonetheless, I cannot say that I regret much, because without these choices, I wouldn't have my beautiful daughter.

So I've had a first career, a white dress, then a Wallis blue one, then a baby. There's no more ticking clock. It's time to have fun and move past my shame. I've faced that shame. I was in a bar and a guy asked if I was married and told him I was divorced. "How many times?" he asked.

"Twice," I answered.

"Two-time loser!" he proclaimed.

Cutting remark, but it was strangely freeing. That's exactly the kind of judgment I'd feared and partly what had kept me in a dysfunctional marriage, and now here was my searing putdown and I was still standing. I laughed and said, "Yep!" I realized that if I could just forgive myself, I might clear my own path to some kind of peace.

Who am I anymore? Another question I've been asking myself. I didn't have the easiest start in life. My father abandoned the family when I was an infant, and my mother was mentally ill. I was raised Mormon, but as a teenager broke away from the church, and my sister and I were eventually placed in foster care. From a very early age, I learned how to take care of myself, and at eighteen years old, I boot-strapped it to the Middle East, buying a one-way ticket to Tel Aviv, traveling the Middle East and Europe before eventually finding my way to New York where I attended Columbia University. I went on to have a successful Wall Street career. My life so far has included being a daughter, sister, student, tutor, bus girl, waitress, field hand, factory worker, babysitter, nanny, camp counselor, temp, receptionist, bookkeeper, computer programmer, caregiver for the elderly, kibbutz cook, broadcasting intern, editorial assistant, proofreader, reporter, girlfriend, wife, Wall Street executive, playwright, and mother. Post-second divorce, I couldn't fathom what my next act would be. I didn't know what I wanted anymore other than to be a good parent to Evie, and who was I to myself, anyway? It was difficult to envision a new life, let alone imagine being truly happy again.

Lately, I've been thinking about all of the choices I've made up to this point in life, including my selections in the husband and boyfriend departments. Should I choose differently now?

I've been thinking about how to choose the right person for me today, knowing what I know. How that may or may not happen, because some of it does come down to luck.

I've been thinking that the partner we might choose for ourselves in our twenties and thirties, around the time that we're looking to get married and perhaps start a family, may be a different person than the one we might choose in our forties or fifties and beyond. The man or woman to grow old with.

I've been thinking that you cannot make good decisions for yourself unless you've explored, tried, failed, succeeded, and have developed a solid sense of self. Until your identity is intact, it's difficult to pick the right partner for you, let alone figure out what makes you happy. I've realized that much of the human experience is comprised of a "to-do" list of "shoulds" that are supposed to make us happy. Then later, we may be shocked when we discover the shoulds may not bring happiness, after all. Marriage is a classic example. When you consider that more than fifty percent of marriages end by year five, it's clearly not working for a large percentage of us. Still, most of us must choose our mates when our identity is still developing. Biology sets us up: – if we want to have children, we must roll the dice and dive into marriage and family. We feel the pressure from parents and peers to settle down and have children, not to mention the fear that if we don't get with "the program," we'll be left behind.

I've also been thinking about the importance of love—in all areas of life: the love of self, family, friends, and romantic love, of course. We need to keep our minds and hearts open, no matter how many times we've been disappointed and betrayed, no matter how much scar tissue layers our hearts. We have to fight against cynicism. To love and be loved is one of the greatest of human needs and joys. Nothing can make us as fulfilled, or in its absence, as empty.

With the benefit of this one-hundred date experiment, I see that Joan was right that this love-life business is at least partly a numbers game. Sure, you could win the lottery and meet your perfect person on Date #1. But it's unlikely, so it makes sense to improve your odds by getting out there and meeting as many people as you possibly can, and in roughly a hundred dates, it's likely you *will* meet someone decent. And meeting someone decent just gets you out of the starting gate. Then you have to see if you can move toward love and partnership with this person. As you read on, you'll see that I met someone by Date #3 who I really fell for, however, the feeling wasn't entirely mutual. If you're really lucky, you'll find someone you love and who loves you back. And if you're exceptionally fortunate, maybe it will stick for a long time. Even a lifetime.

Joan was funny and flip about it, but this dating stuff isn't easy. You're going to break hearts, and your heart will be broken too—at least once. And as one of my dates once commented, "It's hard to date without lying." I think that's right, without lying to others or ourselves. It's among the most noble of challenges to allow new people into our lives, to trust and remain open-hearted.

The good news, though, is that, to some extent, dating is a set of skills you can learn so it gets easier. You will start to recognize at the onset certain key indicators. As Maya Angelou said, "The first time someone shows you who they are, believe them." Relationships demand precious time and energy, so it's important to bravely screen upfront.

Time and again, I'm reminded that it's important to focus on what people do, rather than what they say. Actions, absolutely, speak louder than words.

I've learned a lot. Such as . . . don't chase animal, vegetable, or mineral or it'll break into a run. Like the book and the film *He's Just Not That into You*. Yup. Everything there is glaringly obvious and true to me . . . now.

Don't fall in love with potential; fall in love with what is right here in front of you. The what is, not the what could be. Try to see as clearly as you can. I've done dumb things like fall hard for a man who was separated from his wife, promised to finalize his divorce and still, years later, our relationship remained in purgatory, officially unofficial. Invest in people who marry their promises with action.

Don't make excuses for people, and know that someone who wants to be in your life will perform heroic acts to be with you if they're into you. After two marriages and a lot of dating now, I know. They will come up with any reason to throw themselves in your path. You have a meeting in New York? Oh, guess what, he does too! What a coincidence. Wait? Don't you live four hours away? Sure enough, this suitor eventually admitted to me that his meeting was just a ruse to be able to take me out to dinner. If someone really cares for you, there's no ambiguity: you won't be left guessing about his or her feelings.

As a friend told me once, "Look for a consistency of effort, otherwise it's a mindfuck." If the feelings are mutual, the effort expended—from both sides—will be in balance. Trust your intuition. Does it feel right? You won't need to force, pressure, or demand. In the beginning, hang back, watch, and learn and try to think long-term versus short-term happiness. I've learned not to take a single day for granted. Don't waste time, and don't let other people waste yours, either.

There are so many wonderful permutations of human out there, and it continues to fascinate me. Getting out there and meeting as many people as you can creates opportunities for love, friendship, and other enrichment. Each person you meet can bring you closer to understanding what you're looking for in a partner.

Sometimes dating will be gut-wrenching and other times exhilarating. And as you go, you must think, yet not overthink. For me, overthinking comes naturally, and since love has failed me in the past, I have to work hard to trust myself and the process. I'm still haunted by a male friend who said, "Holly, you're a bad picker!" He then added that men will try to get away with anything they can, so be careful, he warned. It's like the rat in a lab experiment. Don't allow the person you're dating to have you on a random, intermittent reinforcement schedule. Stop pushing the bar, don't be a rat.

Some guys do think they can order up a woman anytime day or night, like a pizza (switching similes from rats to pizza!). Cell phones, dating apps, and tech normalizes that behavior, but don't stand for it. You're worth planning for, asking out in advance, you're worth courting. If you're sharing a bed with someone, you have a right to understand the bigger picture, to ask questions and feel safe and secure. Sometimes men will try to manipulate, deceive, slut-shame consciously or subconsciously, and put their psychological crap on you. Don't give away your power. You always have options. I once dated a man who was super sweet and supportive when sober but an angry, cruel drunk under the influence. When I broke up with him after his drunken, angry rage, he told me it was all my fault that we were parting because I was a "phony" and "damaged." Months later, as he was going through Alcoholic Anonymous's Twelve Steps, he reached out to apologize. It was him, he admitted, and he told me he was sorry. Again, it comes back to your gut, and most of the time, you just know whether a relationship is right or not.

I've learned, too, to make allowances for when my decision-making might be a bit compromised, so I check in with myself to see where I'm falling on that self-esteem versus loneliness spectrum. I try to recognize when I might be at risk to make a foolish choice simply because I'm achingly lonely and/or itching for close, ahem, male contact. I try to stay centered and positive, understanding that there's no way to know what life will throw me next, only that I have the strength to deal with whatever happens.

There's validity to the idea that you'll probably know in the first two minutes or so if you're attracted to someone and then you go from there. A little longer—one date. And if it seems promising, you keep going.

My sense is that by the third date, you will know if there's serious potential. If you still don't know by then, it may be time to move on. And moving on is perfectly okay. "Have a nice life," one of my former dates wished me. And while that can be awkward and painful, it's unavoidable. So just put on your Adult Underpants and gently tell the truth so everyone can move on, dignity intact.

Dating is about coming together and sometimes saying goodbye. And there's a delicate dance of choosing versus being chosen. If you're a woman, you're Ginger Rogers doing everything backwards, in heels, anticipating. Of course, you must choose the dance partner who is right for you, but if you're a woman, I do think you have to let the man ask for that first dance. Dating is both a dance and a negotiation. And if your beloved has decided to no longer tango, determine if it's worth fighting for, and if it isn't, gracefully let go. To gracefully let go. I'm still working on that.

Even being told that a relationship has ended isn't a given anymore. A friend of mine recently complained about being "ghosted"—where someone is in your life hot and heavy and then, without notice, they simply disappear. (That's not a ghost, it's an asshole.) But to the extent you can, let go. Accept that sometimes some things are unknowable and be grateful for what was, without expectation for more. Let go or be dragged, as the Buddhists say.

Why do people love each other and why do they let go? The answer to that is complex. I don't think we get to choose who we care for, let alone love. And perhaps we let go of people who hurt or threaten us in some way. Maybe they rattle our psychological cages, perhaps they're inconstant and let us down or no longer meet our needs. Everything is always changing, including us. We humans tend to gravitate toward pleasure and positivity, eventually letting go of the people and things that bring us pain. Loyalty, commitment, vows, are the antidote to life's flux, but each of us get to decide for ourselves the distance we'll go with a partner, whether it be a week, a year, or a lifetime.

It's easy to get comfortable in a relationship and fall asleep at the switch. To take someone for granted, even yourself, so you need to remain aware, asking yourself the relevant questions. Do you and your beloved bring out the best in each other and are your needs being met? And maybe the biggest question is whether you can maintain your identity and pursue your best life within the relationship.

I see now that who we chose for a partner is often about who we are at a particular point in time. Case in point: the timing of my second marriage, on the heels of my first divorce, just as my biological clock was ticking. I was operating from a place of fear. Your unique, personal history imprints you. For me, I will probably always carry the echo of my former religion and growing up without my father and my mother's view of me as the awkward girl who will never get a date. I know now, of course, that's no longer me or the woman I've become. I understand now how love in adulthood almost always references our earliest loves, our parents, others we loved in childhood. As I discovered in writing this book, the allure of tall, square-jawed, emotionally unavailable older men is probably because my biological father was absent as I grew up. Maybe subconsciously I was trying to salve that psychological wound.

I'm still dating, and these days I'm more confident with it. Experience helps. I think it's time we lose the stigma of women going out alone. Twice in the last few years, I've been asked if I was a prostitute simply because I was out eating dinner alone. Our society is highly uncomfortable with unpartnered people, particularly women.

If you want to go out in the world to do anything—eat a meal, hit a bar, drive a car, take a trip—do it. Do it alone, with five friends, ten children, a partner, whomever—do what makes you happy. And to hell with the judgments that you might be "looking for something." Yes, you're looking for something, you're looking to live your life, as is your right, whether you're a woman or a man.

You get up, you pull yourself together, maybe you even put on a little lipstick. You go out into the world and the rest of the story is up to you.

♥

CHAPTER 2

Clueless and Back in the Saddle

Date #1: Disarming Honesty

His name is Chavez McCormick, and he wants to have a drink.

My online dating profile is up and running and the winks, emails, and date requests are coming in. A fire chief. A twenty-eight-year-old delivery guy. A business professor turned medical student. A thoughtful text from a lawyer. I'm open-minded about who I might date, and I'm not judging anyone based on age, race, profession, or income. The right man could be almost anyone.

I text Luke, my best friend, who's an excellent sounding board on everything, especially dating because he's been doing it most of his adult life. Luke is gay, and we met at my first job. Like me, he also attended Columbia, had a strict, religious mother, and sometimes behaves like an adolescent boy. When I married the second time, Luke stood up for me and I called him my maid of honor just to irritate him.

Me: Date tonight! Back in the saddle.
Luke: How'd you meet?
Me:Online.
Luke: Don't forget to bring an extra cell phone.
Me: Why?
Luke: To call. For when he locks you in the trunk of his car.
Me: Drama. Queen!
Luke: Cars are standard equipped with trunk release latch. You'll be fine. What's his name?
Me: Don't worry about it.
Luke: WHAT'S HIS NAME?
Me: Chavez.
Luke: Bahaha! That dude will definitely lock you in the trunk.

Personal safety concerns aside, what I really need to figure out is what to wear. I've read somewhere that when dating you need a go-to outfit or two. A uniform.

This idea makes sense to me, because I tend to gain and lose the same five pounds so there's times when I cannot fit into certain pairs of pants. These are hung in my closet's Camel Toe section. But this insecurity is a total waste of time. I just need a couple of outfits that will do the job no matter my mood or "situation."

As I dress for the evening, I find myself feeling meh. I'm fighting myself. What the hell am I doing dating at the age of almost forty-five? I never thought I'd be here. There's a slight residue of sleaze and some form of guilt; I almost feel a tiny bit dirty. Marriage and motherhood felt pure and sanctioned.

But I head out the door anyway, and as I walk toward the restaurant in the dim light of the early evening, I see a broad-shouldered man in a long, black coat standing by the door. "Are you Holly?" he asks.

He's got presence. Like a big Viking, he's got piercing blue eyes and wavy white hair. His profile says he went to Princeton. He must have some smarts.

Inside, the bar is wood-paneled and softly lit. There's a TV flickering with a hockey game. We settle onto bar stools and smile a little shyly at each other. "What would you like to drink?" he asks. The bartender comes by, and Chavez gets me a glass of red wine and a club soda for himself.

Interesting. He doesn't drink. Is he a recovered alcoholic?

We talk about our children. I tell him about my daughter, Evie, and Chavez tells me about his three daughters: Bettina, Delphine, and Pera. "Beautiful names," I say, and we chat for awhile about our girls because it's an icebreaker that puts us at ease, yet it's not entirely benign—I sense that there's also the serious question, lurking in the background, for both of us, as to whether our families could compatibly blend. It seems a conversation that every dating parent will naturally have early on.

We swap stories about our childhoods. His father was a quarterback in the NFL. "Well that explains the broad shoulders," I say. This son of a quarterback belongs to a rowing club where he works out most mornings and races on weekends. I tell him that I'm training to run my first half-marathon.

"Were you always a runner?"

"God, no!" I say, laughing at the memory of coming in last in pretty much every grade-school race. "I've always hated it. Until now," and then I think of Zach and my stomach falls. He was the one who got me started. Inspired me with the stories of his Ironmans. Two months ago, I signed up for my first half-marathon and he was proud.

"When is your race?" Chavez asks.

"The end of May."

I study his face for a minute. It's kind and open and he's easy to talk to.

"Can I ask why you and your wife aren't together anymore?"

Chavez sighs softly and looks down at the floor and shrugs. "Money. I never made enough, according to her. I did in the beginning, but then the business took a turn for the worse and there wasn't much I could do. I had to let people go. And she's got . . . let's say . . . some mental health issues."

"Oh."

Chavez looks me in the eye. "And she would say I drank too much."

I nod. "Okay. Any truth in that . . .?"

"Perhaps," he says, smiling.

I smile, too. "Well, it looks like that's behind you now."

"Yes," he says, lifting his glass in a toast and taking a sip of water. His honesty is compelling. "Are you hungry?"

"You know, I am."

"Would you join me for dinner?" he asks.

Over mashed potatoes and pork chops, he tells me he's reading Carl Jung; that Jung believed people never fully grow up until their forties. "I've been thinking the same thing," I say.

After dinner, we walk briskly in the foggy night toward my car, and beneath a street lamp he reaches out his arms and I find myself wanting to be wrapped in them. He gives me a peck on the lips. "Would you like to go out again?" he asks.

"I would."

"Drive safely," he says.

Maybe Chavez will grow on me the way both of my husbands did; a slow smolder that eventually burst into flame.

♥

Date #2: Pre-Ask & Prescreening

This date has been prescreened. Before Bernard asked me out, he suggested we schedule a time to speak by phone first. It was a thinly veiled interview, ensuring I was up to snuff.

Bernie is a partner at a law firm in New Jersey. Patents and intellectual property law are his specialty.

We agree to meet in the city for dinner, and Bernie has pulled out the stops. He has selected Marea, arguably a top-notch Italian seafood restaurant in New York. I'm impressed by his attention to detail (my online profile says how much I love Italy).

I arrive a little early and sit up at the bar and order a drink. A few sips in, I receive a text: "I'm here!" I turn around and there's Bernie, leaning somewhat dramatically against a pillar, his trench coat draped across his buttressing forearm.

My first thought is that his skin is just so *translucent*. Like he's been polished. A head like a candled egg. He looks almost nothing like his online photo.

I stand. "Bernie," I say, reaching my hand for his. I'm so much taller than Bernie. *Didn't his profile say that he was five-foot-eleven? Yeah, he lied.*

"I need a drink!" Bernie proclaims, striding up to the bar.

Bernie has ordered a scotch on the rocks and begins drinking thirstily. "Ahhh . . . I've been in court all day."

"How did that go?"

And then Bernie proceeds to give a detailed, blow-by-blow reenactment of two days of court proceedings, starring Bernie, peppered with intricate patent law detail.

After a time, we are seated for dinner. The dining room is elegant and gilded, the service exacting. There will be multiple courses. This dinner will be long.

The food, as it comes in course after course, is truly delicious, and the champagne and the wines that Bernie selects—he's knows what he's doing—they're exquisite. He talks about his ex-wife and the problems in his marriage. She was somewhat needy is the takeaway.

"Have you been dating much?" I ask.

"To be honest, Holly, not so much. I am very selective. I go for quality over quantity. . . . And as you know, I prescreen . . ."

"Yes, you do."

"I was in a two-year relationship with a woman. A very nice woman. For a while, it did get quite serious."

"Oh," I say. "What happened?"

"Our problems really began around the time she made the decision to have her gastric bypass surgery."

Gastric bypass?

And then the conversation turns to the subject of gastric bypass, the medical considerations, his ex-girlfriend's struggle with her weight and self-esteem, Bernie's efforts to help her. Next it's onto Bernie's own struggles with obesity. He's lost a lot of weight, he says proudly, since he's started running. At least fifty pounds. Over dessert, Bernie tells me he knows when people are thinking of him. E.S.P. I nod politely. *Does he know what I'm thinking right now?*

The waiter presents a silver platter of petit fours and places it in the center of the table. *We are never getting out of here.*

"Holly, there's something I would like to ask you."

"Yes . . .?"

Bernie looks into my eyes. And I, into his. "After dinner is over, and we leave the restaurant, I'm wondering if I might be able to kiss you good night."

"Oh . . ."

"Yes," he says, nodding.

"You want to know now? Alright. Umm. I guess that would be okay."

Oh my God! Why did I just agree to that?

I don't know, I just want to get this whole thing over with!

Outside the restaurant, I'm standing in the street, looking for a cab. *Get. Me. Out. Of. Here!* Bernie steps up on to the curb next to me. We're closer in height now. But I'm still taller. He leans in for the kiss, and I pinch my lips together.

In the car home, I receive a text. "Thanks for a wonderful evening, Sugar."

Sugar?!

♥

CHAPTER 3

Alarm Bells

"Mom! Mom! What's that noise?"

An alarm is going off. It's early morning, and Evie is standing at my bedside, yanking my arm. "Let me check," I croak, slipping on a bathrobe and heading down the hall in the direction of the noise, toward the basement. I turn on lights. It's not the smoke detector. Carbon monoxide, maybe? I don't know. I don't know any of this stuff. This is one of the worst things about being a newly single parent: home maintenance. I keep learning the hard way, like when I forgot to close the garage door on one of the coldest nights of the year and the pipes froze, then burst, flooding the garage and family room. I never wanted this house in the first place, way out in the woods in the middle of nowhere. Can't wait to put it on the market. Now the phone is ringing. The alarm company. They've just dispatched the fire department.

"Fire department? Isn't that overkill?"

"Sorry, ma'am, have to ensure you're safe." Now I can hear the wail of fire trucks in the distance.

I haven't even had coffee yet. "Evie, get dressed!"

"Why?"

"We're going to have visitors. Any second." I dash back to my room to put on some clothes.

"Mom! Mom!" Evie is yelling again.

"What?"

"Get your red dress on! The fire department is coming!"

Evie stands at the front door in a long, red lace skirt and yellow rain boots, looking like a cross between a duck and a Flamenco dancer. She shakes each firefighter's gloved hand as they clomp through our living room in rescue helmets, metal tanks strapped to their backs. "Good morning . . . good morning. . . . I'm well, thank you, how are you? My name is Evie . . ."

The fire department checks everything and determines it's a false alarm. I just have to remember to change the alarm batteries. Learning to be alone again. Of course I can do this. What choice do I have?

I get Evie on the school bus and finally have that cup of coffee. Birth and death, marriage and divorce. Divorce feels like a death of sorts, except the person who died is still walking the earth. I am grieving the loss of the man who was my closest ally, the death of a long-held dream of a happy, intact family. I know I need to pull myself together and force myself onward.

And moving on means bringing new people into my life. I promise myself that when Evie is with her father and I'm solo, I will get out as much as possible. I will network with former colleagues, explore my interests, and when hungry, eat out. I will try new restaurants, dining alone, if need be. Almost every restaurant has a bar where they will serve you dinner. I will bring a book and my phone as company, and I'll sit back and see what happens. I can do this. I'm accustomed to doing things on my own, taking action, pulling my life out of a nosedive, saving myself. I've done it before.

And enough stewing. It's time to start packing. We're heading to California tomorrow for Evie's spring break. A little California sunshine should boost the morale, as my grandmother used to say.

Next day we fly, head to our beach house there and settle in.

♥

Date #3: I'll Be a Gentleman

It's a Saturday night in Cali, and I've booked a babysitter so I can have a few hours to myself. Evie is happy to stay home.

I pull on some jeans, a white T-shirt, and a black leather jacket, some lipstick, too, and head to a new restaurant near the waterfront. The place is hopping.

I weave through the crowd to the middle of the bar and squeeze past a tall, silver-haired man, also wearing a leather jacket, who is waiting, too. I order wine and tell the bartender that I'd like to eat at the counter. I stand there with my drink, waiting, and right next to me is the silver-haired man. I stare straight ahead, and it's awkward since we're so close that we're almost touching and I think I feel him looking at me. I glance over. *What a handsome man.* He has large blue eyes and chiseled features. At least six-foot-two. *But he's too old for me. Probably in his sixties.*

I look at my phone. *Anything from the babysitter?* All quiet.

"I feel like I should introduce myself. I'm Jack," the man says in a very deep voice. *Whoa. That voice.*

I offer my hand, which becomes lost in his. He has a riveting gaze and I tell him my name. "Do you live in town?" I ask.

"No, Boston. Here for a conference. How about you?"

I tell him about my beach house and Connecticut.

"I'm in New York a lot. I used to live there," he says. And just then, the two people seated in front of us get up to leave so Jack and I sit down together, and the bartender wipes the counter and lays out placemats and hands us menus. We fall quiet as we read. He's pulled out some black-framed reading glasses, and I think how I've always liked a handsome man in glasses.

"What looks good to you?" Jack asks. The bartender assumes that we're together and takes our order at the same time. "How long are you here for?" Jack says.

I explain that it's my daughter's spring break and that I'm divorced. "How about you," I say. "Are you married?"

Jack gives a little laugh. "Nope. No kids, never married."

"You're the George Clooney of Boston!"

Jack laughs again. "I came close," he says. "Engaged. Have been in an on-again-off-again relationship for fourteen years. It's off now."

As we eat our dinner, we share a little food off each other's plates. He tells me that his father passed away four months ago after a long battle with Parkinson's. His mood has changed. "I'm sorry," I say. "That must be very hard." And then he mentions that his mother is a writer.

"A writer!" I tell him what I do.

I find myself at ease in this man's presence, and when he tells me that he's the CEO of an investment company, our conversation lights up even more. We've lived similar lives, know some of the same people, speak the same language.

When the bartender brings the check, I realize he's put both meals on one bill. "Let me get this," Jack says, winking, quickly snatching it out of my grasp.

"Well, maybe you'll let me buy you a drink," I say.

"I'd enjoy that."

♥

Outside, the air has a chill. There's a band playing nearby. Jack and I are meandering, side by side, warmed by wine and a good meal. "Where shall we go?" I ask.

"How about in the direction of the music?" Jack says. As we cross the street and turn the corner, he pulls me close and tries to kiss me on the mouth.

I literally step back. "You're a little forward," I say sharply.

"I'm sorry. I do love a tall, thin, blonde," he says without the slightest hint of guilt. He smiles and tugs me by the arm, and I see that he has a small gap between his front teeth. A tall, thin, blonde. *What am I, a type to him? Of course, I always love a handsome man in glasses.*

At the bar, people are dancing to a live band. I ask Jack what he'd like to drink, and he smiles a little apologetically and I soften. We take our drinks and decide to sit in a small room out of the way where it's quieter, so we can talk.

We sit down on a weather-beaten sofa and almost roll into each other's laps. We start laughing. The sofa is more like a waterbed. "I'll be a gentleman," Jack says, and then he kisses me again, and this time I kind of like it. "It's been a long time since I've been kissed," he says, leaning back, staring up at the ceiling, as though he's gone somewhere else for a moment.

"Really? I don't know if I believe that," I say.

Soon I tell him I want to leave and I catch a cab home. Within minutes, my phone rings. It's him. He asks if we can see each other again and I say, "I'd like that."

♥

The next day, I'm at the gym, running on the treadmill training for my marathon, feeling thirsty and hazy, wondering why it was a good idea to drink the night before. I think about Jack. I find him intriguing, yet I'm skeptical. A man so handsome and charming, sixty years old and never married? It suggests commitment phobia, yet he did say he had been in a fourteen-year relationship.

I keep running. I'm clocking the miles. I'm starting to feel better and then a text comes in:

> At LAX.
> I trust all is well at your house this morning.
> Karma was smiling on me last night. J
> Speak soon,
> Jack

I crank up the speed on the treadmill and run faster. I find myself smiling.

♥

Bernie has been texting me every few days, and I've been politely answering. He hasn't asked me out again, so I figure it's okay to be friendly.

> **Bernie**: I have to tell you about my weekend! I had the most amazing experience. I went to a wolf sanctuary.

Me: Cool.

Bernie: One wolf in particular. She looked into my eyes and I looked into hers and there was a bond.

Me: Wow.

Bernie: So moving. I made a presentation about her.

Me: Presentation?

Bernie: Yes. For the partners of my law firm.

For the partners of your law firm. Luke is gonna love this. ESP and now wolf bitch bonding. Then, a week and a half later, another text:

Bernie: Hard to believe my last exchange with you was over 10 days ago. Was tempted to call but figured I would have heard from you by now if there was interest. Hope you are doing well.

Crap. Now what? I get Luke on the phone, and he coaches me on composing a kind, clear, and direct reply:

Hi Bernie, you've been on my mind and apologies for not being in contact sooner. I really enjoyed meeting you, but definitely feel we are better suited as friends. Wishing you all the best. Take care.

A few hours pass and then Bernie replies:

Okay. Disappointed that you didn't share this with me before, but so be it. Common in the dating world, I suppose. Have a great life, Holly.

Common. Have a great life. Ouch.

♥

CHAPTER 4

Happy Birthday, Quasimodo

It's Monday, and I've been back on the East Coast fewer than twenty-four hours when Jack calls. He's going to be in New York this week. Do I want to have dinner on Wednesday night in the city?

I tell him I wish I could, but can't, and don't offer an explanation. I don't say that I have Evie and that I'd rather spend the time with her. I suggest lunch on Thursday instead, when she's with her father. Jack says he cannot do lunch. "That's alright, maybe another time," I say. That is that.

Later that day, Jack texts to say that he's changed his schedule for me. He's now available for lunch and has selected a restaurant. I recognize it immediately. It's in the same building where I worked for years in my Wall Street days. The building with the view of Central Park. The building of my old life. The building where I worked when I met Evie's father.

♥

Date #4: Not Quite Bizniss

I enter the New York City restaurant I've dined in many times before. Back then, I entertained clients or lunched with colleagues, but this time I'm on a date. It feels strange, and I'm a little on edge. The restaurant is filled with business people immersed in conversation, their voices rising into the space flooded with sunshine from floor-to-ceiling windows.

In years past, I might wear a navy suit and pearls, but today I have on a fitted gray, flannel dress with leather capped sleeves and high heel gray pumps.

The maître d' leads me to the table, and when Jack sees me, he stands. Thick silver hair, ice blue eyes, a dark suit and tie. Move over, James Bond. "Hello, Holly," he says in that baritone, kissing my cheek, his hand at the small of my back.

We make a little weather talk, and I find the conversation flows less easily than in California. We are both feeling the formality of the setting, perhaps. We're drinking sparkling water instead of wine. He is in New York for two days of meetings and another conference.

Who is this perpetual bachelor of Boston?

I ask if he's ever lived with someone before, and instantly there's more discomfort. "Yes. For a time," he says, the tone guarded, almost with a hint of warning to pull back, like brushing a hot pot on a stove.

At his age—sixty, almost sixty-one—to have never been married . . . to have never shared your toys . . . There's a story with this man and the on-again-off-again woman of fourteen years.

And yet, I'm attracted to him and already know I want to see him again.

Outside, we stand looking at each other in the early spring sunshine as the lunch-time rush of Midtown swirls around us. He leans in and gives me a long, deep kiss and grabs my ass. *In the middle of Midtown!* He can see the surprise on my face and gives me a big grin as he walks away, a broad-shouldered silhouette in his tailored suit, there's a little swagger, and then I lose sight of him in the shadow of skyscrapers.

I feel my face warm, knowing I'm blushing. Waiting for the light at Fifth Avenue, I recognize a man waiting, too—someone I knew from years ago.

"Lou?"

He smiles at me. Another handsome, older, blue-eyed man. He's the CEO of my former firm, the self-made billionaire I used to travel with on the company jet for client presentations. I can tell he's struggling to recall my name; it's been more than seven years. "Holly . . ." I say, and he remembers.

Another vestige of my past, a life that feels lost. Seeing Lou leaves me with an emptiness I'm not sure I understand. I find myself embarrassed at the thought of Lou seeing Jack kiss me like that and then chide myself for caring. He didn't even remember my name. That time in my life is gone. So who am I now, feeling a garble of emotions, from hope to sadness?

From the train, I text Jack and thank him for lunch and tease him about the kiss and the gratuitous grab. He texts back immediately, flirty. I hope I'll see him again.

♥

There's another part of my life that I'm working on: creating a home. To find a home that I love, a home of my choosing.

Since my former husband, David, and I moved back to the United States after a six-year hiatus abroad, I've been living in the woods of rural Connecticut in a house I never wanted. From the moment I set foot in the place, something felt off. Bad juju, isolation, hard to put my finger on it. We were under pressure to buy something because David thought he might lose his job. We argued heatedly and he insisted we buy that house and eventually we did.

The house was symbolic of our disconnect: I had gone from respecting his opinion, admiring his brilliant thinking, and appreciating his benevolent leadership in our marriage to feeling steamrolled, always placating, afraid of infuriating him. Fearful of another argument and what it might mean for us, because we were fragile. The Connecticut house became the final stage for the unraveling of our marriage.

I decide that I will sell this albatross and buy in another town—one closer to New York City, a town where Evie has access to some of the best schools. We will make new memories and begin a life that is completely our own.

I find a real estate agent and begin my search. We're driving at break-neck speed in the agent's Range Rover down I-95, two months' worth of discarded coffee cups and Slim-Fast cans flying through the air. She's a forty-something woman with a passion for hats in any weather and QVC shopping. "So, you're divorced, huh?" she says. "I'd get divorced, too, but I'm just too lazy."

I crack up. "Just too lazy, huh?"

"Yeah, it's too much work, so I stay," she says, grinning. "And remind me—there's someone I want to set you up with."

Some of the truest things are said in jest.

After a couple days of legwork, I start to understand that I want to buy in a particular waterside town where I can walk to shops and restaurants and Evie and I will have a little community. I want to be able to walk to the train station that takes me into New York, where we will no longer be isolated. I begin to have a vision of how our new life should be.

I will raise Evie in a place where we have friends. A community of friends we build, one good person at a time, blended together with the old friends we've loved for years.

I want Evie to grow up in a comfortable, loving, relaxed home. Where she has room to be a kid, to go to a school where she's appreciated for who she is and can test and develop her talents.

A home where there's always room for one more at the table, a place filled with laughter and friends and good food and warmth.

I want to show Evie how to live—how to be happy—how oftentimes we have to consciously work for our own happiness.

How every day there needs to be time for both work and play—balance.

A life of intention. A life that we shape according to what matters most.

Evie is watching. I am teaching her what it means to be a person, a woman, a mother. How to be true to yourself.

♥

It's morning. I have one eye open. A remote-control helicopter is flying through my bedroom. Evie has taped a sign to it. "Happy Birthday!" it says.

"It worked!" she says, jumping up and down with a thud. "Happy birthday, Mom!" She maneuvers the helicopter to the floor. Zach taught her to fly that thing.

I am forty-five years old.

Evie bounds onto my bed. She's in her orange and black Halloween pajamas covered in bats that she likes to wear year-round. Her hair is a tangled mop. She's brought her ratty rabbit cuddle toy we call Hop and she holds it close when she sucks her thumb. Hop was once pink but is now gray from dirt, love, and God knows what else. Evie cuddles in next to me, proudly presenting a homemade card with hearts, flowers, and rainbows. Inside, she's drawn a cake with a lot of flaming candles on it—I suspect precisely forty-five (the girl has an eye for detail)—and she's written, too, how much she loves me. How lucky am I?

She hands me a gift-wrapped package: inside, a book on yoga. "Do you like it?" she asks. "It was my idea!"

"It's perfect," I say, putting an arm around her and pulling her close. She still smells like my little baby. And this isn't just a birthday gift from Evie; it's also a gift from David, and an olive branch. The gesture is quite unexpected, and I realize he's signaling a desire to work together as coparents. He's solidly in Evie's life now, ironically, more involved, a more hands-on a father than when we were married. I'm grateful that Evie knows her father in a way that I never knew mine.

Later in the day, I go to the city and spend a leisurely afternoon shopping until I meet Luke and other friends for dinner.

I'm in Soho, in a clothing store changing room tangled in a Diane Von Furstenberg wrap dress, when my phone rings. It's Jack. I let it go to voice mail.

Once I leave the store, I listen, my pulse quickening, and in the deepest, most gravely voice, I hear "Happy Birthday, you beautiful girl, you," and he hangs up.

My God. Maybe the sexiest message ever.

♥

Date #5: DeNiro is My Homeboy

To this date, I shuffle like Quasimodo. I've got so many blisters from my half-marathon training I can barely walk, let alone put on pretty shoes. Evie calls them my "hamburger feet."

And feet are a focus for Ivan, my mystery date, because we start off on the wrong foot. When he emails and asks how he'll recognize me, I joke "Short, dark, with a limp." He takes me literally and wants to back out, so I have to smooth things over by reassuring him that I am indeed blonde and tall. No sense of humor. Strike one.

Ironically, Ivan is the shorter one, with dark hair to boot, and looks older than his online photo by at least a decade. Over a drink, he's quick to say that he's friends with Robert DeNiro and a producer of the world's major film festivals.

Ivan's convinced that he knows within the first *two minutes* of a date whether or not it's going to work out with a woman. I decide, on the spot, that perhaps he's exactly right.

We talk about writing, feminism, his emasculating *wife* (he lied online, he admits; they are newly separated, not divorced). The unapologetic, open admission of lying is troubling. We drink our wine, and the hour together is not unpleasant. But when we say goodbye, I know that we'll never see each other again. And that seems the best outcome for us both.

♥

Date #6: Can Somebody Send Me a Sign?

Second date with Chavez at a suburban bistro with black and white tile, red leather barstools.

We eat at the bar leaning into each other, shoulder to shoulder, talking quietly, about the day's events, our kids, more Jung, and rowing. Chavez exudes a steady warmth and is so companionable that, when dinner is over, I'm sorry to say good night. But as I drive home, I realize I'm confused. Chavez tests Ivan's Two-Minute Theory. With Chavez, there's no butterflies, but no red flags, either.

Eh. More research needed. More dates.

♥

CHAPTER 5

Thirty-One Flavors of Freak

Date #7: I Scream, You Scream, We All Scream for Tofu Scallion Spread

Online, there's an athletic-looking guy who keeps after me—when can we get together, Kyle wants to know. Huge biceps, full head of thick, blonde hair, big, perfect smile. We are both busy, so we decide to talk on the phone first. We settle on an early morning call, which I take in a taxi from New York City en route to LaGuardia.

"Good morning!" Kyle says.

"You're up early!" I say.

"Want to know why?"

"Sure."

"I'm going to send you a video. Can you watch it on your phone?" Kyle says.

"Okay . . ." *Wait—is this some sick setup? What type of video?*

"I just sent it!"

After I hang up with Kyle, I watch his video. There is no naked flesh, only bagels. Kyle is the king of bagels and he has an empire.

He is talking to me in the video. He's showing me his cream cheese and he does a close-up of each type. "Vegetable . . . tofu-scallion . . ." The camera pauses on an empty metal bin. "Sold out of the strawberry cream cheese. *Ohhh boy!* Gonna have to get some downstairs—*RUSH!*" he screams to someone off-camera, unhinged, like it's a life-and-death emergency. And in that moment, I know that a guy who becomes apoplectic over toppings for boiled dough is probably not the guy for me. I text him:

> Hi Kyle. Thanks for the chat. I enjoyed it but don't feel that requisite spark. Wishing you all the best.
>
> **Kyle**: U2 safe flight.

I'm learning. People like a good bagel. With options and lotsa toppings. They also like honesty.

♥

Date #8: Sixteen and Awkward

Third date with Chavez. The weather is warm, and we stroll over to a nearby park where we sit on a bench beneath a large, shady oak and eat our over-stuffed tuna sandwiches and potato chips.

We have another engaging conversation, but I'm beginning to feel like an awkward sixteen-year-old around him—self-conscious, as though I've lost my bearings. Is this because I like him and this could turn into something, or am I just afraid to bridge the physical part of our relationship because deep down I don't think it will work? And yet, as we say goodbye after our picnic lunch, we make plans to see each other again. What am I going to do?

And still, I think about Zach. I haven't been physically intimate with anyone since our breakup. Will I ever be able to find another relationship where the physical was as nearly flawless and in synch as it was with him?

The thought of sharing my body with someone new both thrills and threatens me. While I'm mature enough to understand that sex is as natural as breathing, I know, for me, that it changes things. I become more vulnerable. Once I care for a man and that caring is coupled with a physical relationship, it bonds me to that person in a way that sometimes feels out of control, as though my judgment has been clouded.

Maybe that's what I'm afraid of. Being hurt, vulnerable, losing control. And after what Zach and I have gone through and what I'm still getting over, I wonder if I'm ready.

Luke snaps me out of my mulling with a text:

> Our friendship is the one perfect thing. No matter what, we'll always have each other.

He reminds me that while I haven't always been lucky in love, I've been lucky in life. I have true friends.

♥

Date #9: Beached

An afternoon walk at the beach is Chavez's idea for our fourth date.

The day is sunny, but cool, with a breeze that chases the clouds across the sky and ruffles his white curls. We wear windbreakers and walk along the water's edge.

We fall into step and he takes my hand. There's a ripple of electricity but I notice, too, that I'm having a hard time concentrating. My breath is shallow and I'm feeling almost panicky.

After a time, we climb a hill and settle onto a bench that looks out on Long Island Sound. He picks up my hand again and squeezes it. "Do you like the view?" he asks.

"It's beautiful," I say, staring out at the horizon, following a boat in the distance. "Sorry. I'm really nervous right now."

"Okay." Gently he returns my hand to my lap. He looks a little confused. Or hurt.

"I don't know why. Maybe it's because it's been a while since someone has touched me? Since my boyfriend and I broke up."

"How long has that been?"

I pause to think. "A couple of months now, I guess."

"It's okay. I can be patient," he says.

I stare down at the ground, unsure of what to say next. "Thank you. I don't understand it myself." *What the hell is wrong with me?*

We sit in awkward silence for a few minutes. "Shall we walk back to the car?" he says, finally.

On the way back, I'm able to breathe again. I link my arm through his. "Thank you," I say, giving him a squeeze. *This is a nice man.*

We make plans to see each other again. On Easter Sunday.

♥

Date #10: Big Brains, Bad Libations

Finally meeting Evan. This is Mister Big Pharma Research, Mister PhD big brain. After weeks of texting, we have a first date in the city. He's picked a tapas restaurant in Tribeca, in the neighborhood where he lives.

There he is. Even when seated, you can tell that he's very tall. Wearing a charcoal sport coat with jeans. Dark hair and lots of it; thick, squared, black-framed glasses; high cheekbones; serious expression on his face. He's examining the menu with great intensity.

When I walk over and introduce myself, my first impression is that his voice is booming. But the voice contrasts with Evan's demeanor—he actually seems a little nervous.

Evan immediately suggests that we try tasting some sherries. "Sherry? Okay," I agree, a little puzzled, but amused. *Isn't sherry for gassy old ladies, after dinner?*

We try a flight of four. Each are awful.

We switch to red wine and finally begin to relax. He, too, spends a lot of time in California where he also has a second home. Napa. We talk about California wine.

We linger a long time, and I notice that he touches my arm a lot. Toward the end of the evening, he very smoothly just leans across the table and kisses me on the mouth. He pulls back and studies me. In the dim light, it's hard to see his eyes, but he gives me a sly smile. *Hmm. Not bad.*

And we are funny together. We make each other laugh. He, too, is a parent of a little girl and has an earnestness, an intellectualism, a tiny bit of geek that I find adorable.

"Let me help you find a cab," he says at the end of the evening. He kisses me good night, and I have a pretty good idea that we'll be seeing each other again.

♥

Date #11: Sacrificial Lamb

It's Easter Sunday. By 9:00 a.m., texts are in from Jack, Evan, and Chavez. Happy Easter! What's on the menu? The menu includes roast leg of lamb with mint sauce, I answer. Chavez and I have made plans to have dinner at my house, but I don't tell Jack and Evan that.

Evie is with David for the weekend, and Chavez's daughters are with his ex, so it will be dinner for two. I will cook the lamb and he will bring dessert: his mom's recipe for Texas buttermilk pie.

I've made some effort to get in the spirit of the day. I've planted daffodils and pink and purple hyacinths in the planters at the front of the house, and on the dinner table are candles and lilies.

Chavez arrives wearing a crisply starched mauve dress shirt, smelling of after-shave. Seeing him standing here in my house all eager and squeaky clean is making me aware of how alone we are out here. *Just the two of us. There have been several dates already. Celebrating a holiday. No pressure.*

"How can I help?" he says, carrying his buttermilk pie into the kitchen. "Mmm! Something smells good! Is that rosemary?"

Chavez knows his way around a kitchen. He's adept at washing the butter lettuce and snipping the chives for the salad and whisking the vinaigrette. Music is playing, we're talking up a storm, and I'm having a little wine. Chavez is drinking the lemon-lime seltzer he asked me to buy.

We sit down to dinner, and to my surprise, the lamb turns out beautifully. Juicy with a hint of garlic and rosemary. And then it's onto dessert where he presents his mother's buttermilk pie that has a cracked surface like a dry lakebed. "Mom used to make this all the time. Reminds me of home," he says.

I take a bite and feel his eyes on me, watching, and I force a smile. "Wow, that's . . . so . . . different!" I say, swallowing hard. "Is this some kind of custard?"

And then the meal is done. I stand, smiling, in my skirt and sweater set, and together we bring the plates into the kitchen. At the sink, I rinse the dishes and begin loading the dishwasher. I hear footsteps and Chavez comes up from behind me and places his hands on my shoulders, massaging them roughly. My body stiffens. *Oh no.*

"Let's go sit down," he says in a low tone, pulling my arm.

But I am rooted to the floor. I take a breath. "Okay," I say, trying not to sound as half-hearted as I feel.

He leads me to the blue velvet sofa by the front window. It has grown dark now.

We sit, and suddenly he is kissing me. His tongue is everywhere and down my throat. It's small and pointy and probing.

How did Zach kiss me? It was never like this.

His hands are everywhere. I come up for air.

What direction did Zach's mouth move when mine moved the other way . . .? How? How do you kiss?

I feel Chavez's body. His stomach is soft, he has love handles bulging above his waistband, but his biceps are firm. My mind spins, recalling Zach's chest, the taut muscle, the tri-athlete's body.

My hand brushes Chavez's head. I feel the bare skin of his bald spot, his fine, thinning curls.

Zach's hair was so thick and long. I could grab it by the handful. My friends joked that he looked like Jesus. Jesus, beard and all.

"I'm sorry," I say, sitting tall.

Chavez stops. He moves to the opposite corner of the sofa. "What?" he says.

"You're a sweetheart," I say.

"I'm not sure how to take that."

"As a compliment. I'm sorry, but this doesn't feel right."

"You just need to relax. Let's go to the bedroom . . ." he says, stroking the top of my hand with his finger.

"I'm sorry. No."

"But lovemaking is spiritual . . ." Chavez says seductively.

I almost burst out laughing. "I'm sorry."

Chavez stands and walks briskly to the kitchen. He begins packing up his pie.

"I feel bad about you leaving—with this weirdness," I say.

He doesn't answer.

At the door, he gives me a stiff hug and leaves.

♥

The next morning, I awake and remember the events of the night before and cringe. *So unbelievably awkward.* I bury my head under the pillow. *Argh.*

Finally, I get up and go to the kitchen to make some strong coffee and then crawl right back into bed.

I check my phone. Nothing from Chavez. Did I treat him fairly? Was I fair to myself? I feel so bad. Am I dating too soon after Zach?

What the hell am I doing exactly? Let's return to basics here. Aren't I just looking for one nice boyfriend, where it feels right? I type a memo on my phone:

- Chemistry
- Attractive
- Tall
- Emotionally available
- Wants relationship & makes it a priority
- Good sense of humor
- Intelligent
- Kind
- Good values
- Shared interests
- Financially secure
- Not crazy

This is a long list—is it too much to ask for?

I look again. The only things I could compromise on would be height and financial security. If the guy was truly wonderful and we got along like a house on fire, then the height requirement might melt away. Same for the financial security. Perhaps it should just be "gainfully employed"? If the man were smart and actively pursuing his dream while supporting himself, then that would be fine by me.

But the rest are basics. Chemistry. A decent kisser. You have to *want* to be kissed by the man. Not to feel like you're being suffocated by a large mouth bass.

I get Luke on the phone and tell him what happened.

"Well, of course he's disappointed," Luke says.

"Why do you say that?"

"Anytime you invite a man over to your house for dinner that means you're going to sleep with him."

"What? It does not!"

Luke snorts. "Amateur."

"Get out. Sure, a kiss, a little making out, maybe—but automatic sleepover? No way!"

"In my world, it does! Guys usually give it up by the third date."

"Third date? Well, I never got the memo!" I am shrieking now. "I guess the bases are different in your world. What are the gay bases?"

"First, kissing. Second oral, third butt sex. And a homerun is brunch."

"Brunch?" We roar with laughter. "Why does this have to be so fucking awkward?"

"Ohhh . . . it's okay," Luke says soothingly. "It's okay. You're doing great. Remember, you just work with about three guys at a time, and then you weed them out as you go."

"Last night felt more like a culling. Awful."

After I hang up, I think on it some more. Poor Chavez. The man, and he's a very good one, has been a victim of my inexperience and overthinking. But thank God I didn't sleep with him. As it turns out, Chavez will never call me again.

♥

CHAPTER 6

I Neglected to Mention

Date #12: Cheap Trick

Onward. My second date with Evan in New York, at an Italian restaurant almost entirely illuminated by candlelight. We study our menus, and I ask if he's been dating much.

"You know, you're the best person I've met online."

"Really?" I say, feeling the glow of the compliment.

"Before you, it's been a string of Russian models."

"Models?" *All guys want to date models, remember?*

"It didn't occur to them to pick up a tab—ever," he says.

"Oh." Now I'm unsure what to say. "Is it cultural, maybe?"

"Probably," he says with a hint of bitterness. *Models don't eat much anyway. They're cheap dates!*

But then Evan changes the subject and starts telling me about growing up in upstate New York in a large, close, Catholic family, and he's absolutely charming and I'm starting to like him again after the crass comments he made earlier. I laugh at his tales of sibling rivalry and childhood antics.

Midway through the meal, his demeanor changes again and he says, "There are two things I need to tell you."

I can tell by his expression that this might be serious. "Okay," I say, feeling a little queasy.

"When I was a kid, I used to play a lot of hockey."

"Okay . . ." I smile.

"And one day, we were outside playing in the street and my friend accidently hit me in the eye with a hockey stick."

"Oh God." I shield my eyes in defense of the thought and then study his face, searching for any injury, but just the glow of the candle is reflected in his glasses.

"Doctors tried to save my eye, but they couldn't. They removed it."

"Removed it?"

"I have a glass eye now."

"Oh. I never noticed. You can't even tell."

"You never noticed?"

"No, not really. I thought that maybe you had a slight—just ever so slightly lazy eye or something?" I clear my throat. *Lazy eye. I just said lazy eye. Is that PC? Shit.* "And what is the second thing?"

"I'm still married."

"What?"

"Yes."

"What?" *Still married, glass eye. Still married, glass eye.* "But your online profile says 'divorced'!"

"I know," Evan says sheepishly. "We're separated. The divorce is almost done."

I sit back in my chair. "I don't like this."

"Really. The divorce is almost done. It's very close."

"You lied."

Evan reaches out and brushes my arm. "I was afraid that if I put 'separated,' no one would want to go out with me."

I nod. "That's right. And for good reason. Being separated is quite distinct from being divorced. From not only a legal standpoint, but an emotional one."

Evan crosses his arms. "So, I shouldn't date until my divorce is done?"

"I think you should be upfront and honest about your situation and let the women you date decide for themselves." My statement hangs in the air for a couple of heavy beats.

"That's a good point. I'm sorry."

Later, when the check comes, I pull out my credit card and say, "Let me get this." I'm upset. I want to get home and just sleep on everything.

♥

In the morning, I decide I need to talk things out with Evan.

"Last night was fun," he says, when I call him. "Thank you for dinner."

"You're welcome." *Grrr.* "You know, I need to say something about what you said last night."

"About my eye?"

"Ha!" We laugh a little. "No, not your eye. What bothers me is that you're still married."

"I'd like the chance to explain."

"To me, this is about honesty."

"I get it. Please, just give me a chance to explain my situation. Please go out with me one more time?" He asks so earnestly, and it's this earnestness that has me agreeing to another date by the time I hang up the phone as well as thinking that whatever he has to say had better be good.

Next I text Luke:

Me: Evan confessed two things last night.
Luke: Come at me.
Me: He has a glass eye.
Luke: HOW DID YOU NOT NOTICE HE HAS A GLASS EYE?
Me: It's a very good one?
Luke: YOU DIDN'T SEE ANYTHING? A GLINT, A GLEAM?
Me: He picks dark bars and restaurants.
Luke: Some Oedipal thing?
Me: Not self-inflicted.
Luke: How, then?
Me: Hockey accident.
Luke: Ow.
Me: Right?!
Luke: It's Steve Austin minus the six million dollars. What's the second thing?
Me: He's still married.
Luke: HOW DID YOU NOT KNOW HE WAS STILL MARRIED?
Me: He lied.
Luke: Dump his one-eyed ass!
Me: I'm thinking about it.

♥

Date #13: Just A Matter of Paperwork?

Evan has an hour to make his case. In the Sunday morning sunshine of the restaurant where we meet for brunch, his glass eye is more prominent. Discreetly, I check it out. There's some depth and subtlety to the glass, and the deep brown color matches the other closely. Thumbs-up on the high quality. Over Eggs Benedict, I forget about his "ocular prosthesis" (Google is my friend) and turn my attention to the real issue.

"My wife, Jane, and my daughter, Mella, and I were living in California. I was offered this job in New York and they were supposed to follow me out here," Evan says. "During the move, Jane wants to have a month-long visit with her parents in Ohio so Mella can spend time with the grandparents. Unbeknownst to me, Jane applies for a job at the medical center there as chief of surgery, gets the job, and files for divorce. Says if I want to see Mella, come to Ohio."

"God, I'm sorry."

Evan's mouth twitches. "It's been stressful."

"I can imagine."

"The woman I loved and trusted . . . took away . . ." His voice cracks. ". . . my baby girl." He picks up his phone. "Look at her," he says, staring at a photo of his daughter.

"She's gorgeous." Mella gazes doe-eyed into the camera, awakening from a nap in her crib, tangled in a white blanket.

"Listen . . ." He looks at me intently. "My marriage is truly over; it's just a matter of the final paperwork. I really want to keep seeing you."

His words hang in the air. I think of Zach, what I put him through during my divorce, my roller coaster of emotions. We had a clouded start. "When I started dating, I promised myself that I wouldn't see anyone who was married or in the process of divorcing," I say to Evan. "Because I know firsthand how all-consuming it can be. I need a relationship where my partner has full emotional capacity."

"I get it," Evan says. "I have a very large capacity, you know," he says, smiling suggestively.

"You do, do you?"

"Yep."

We sit there a minute, smiling at each other. "You don't fully understand this yet—but you're going to need time to heal from your divorce," I say. "Divorce is a death of sorts. Deep grieving."

He nods. "But I need to get on with my life, too. Have someone special to share it with. Does that make sense?"

"It does."

"Can I ask you something?" Evan asks.

"Sure."

"What exactly are you looking for?"

His question pulls me back—because the last time someone asked that question, it was David, and the way David had asked hinted that he wanted to marry me.

"What am I looking for? My person. My best friend. Someone special to enjoy life with," I answer quietly.

Evan rests his hand over his heart. "We want the same things, you and I."

I nod.

"So let's not give up on this yet," he says.

He looks like he's going to cry. "That makes sense."

♥

CHAPTER 7

Nightcaps & Presumptions

Date #14: I've Heard That Before

Jack has invited me to dinner. He's driving down from Boston. He makes it sound like he might have some business in New York but the details are hazy. Is he coming just to see me?

Third date. This is a third date! And this man is from out-of-town. Where does he stay? Now that I have the memo on what's supposedly supposed to happen by the third date—if Luke knows anything about what he's talking about—then I need to head this off at the pass. I text Jack:

> **Me**: Let me know if you need hotel recommendations.
> **Jack**: Yes, thanks. Wouldn't want to be presumptuous.
> **Me**: Ha!

Later he lets me know he's staying at my recommended hotel.

As I'm driving to meet him, I realize that I've gone on thirteen dates since the breakup with Zach. And this is the very first time I've been utterly excited to see someone—I actually have butterflies.

I've decided that this will be the night to wear a simple, sleeveless, little black dress.

I enter the lounge of the hotel. The early evening light is soft, and there is a waterfront view of the river and a pianist playing jazz on a baby grand. Standing tall in a navy jacket, among a group of people at the bar, there he is.

Our eyes lock, and he watches me with a smile as I cross the room. My breath becomes short, and suddenly I'm so aware of each and every step that brings me closer to him that I've almost forgotten how to walk. The heels I'm wearing aren't helping.

"Hello, Holly," he says in his low voice and kisses me softly on the mouth. "You look lovely."

His pale blue shirt makes his eyes seem even more blue. My face is warm, and I can't look at him for a second.

While the bartender brings our wine, Jack checks his watch. "A gentleman is supposed to arrive ten minutes early—the lady, ten minutes late. Seems like a giant waste of time, don't you think?"

I laugh. "It's exactly seven," I answer, glancing at my watch. "What does that say about me?"

"It means you're perfect," he says, brushing my arm.

With his hand on my waist, he guides me to a corner where we sit on a red velvet loveseat. We are shoulder to shoulder, arm to arm. Our thighs touch.

He tells me he had lunch today with a former colleague who is buying a house nearby. And then I wonder again about Jack's actual purpose in being here: was it to see the colleague, or me, or both?

I tell him that I've also been looking for a new home. "I think I might have found it—very close to here."

"Good for you," Jack says, and as he talks to me about real estate, it's hard not to be distracted by his body next to mine and the way our limbs have relaxed into each other. When our glasses are empty, he says, "We have a reservation. Shall we?"

Outside, it's warm and the light is gently fading. We meander toward the parking lot. "Do you mind driving?" I say, dangling my keys. "It would be nice to have more than one drink."

"Certainly."

I get in on the passenger side and it's funny to see Jack figuring out how to start my car. I say nothing and just watch. His hands seem enormous on the wheel, and I like this feeling of driving with him, of occupying the same small space. Just driving somewhere together. Regular people. Like a couple.

As we near the restaurant, I say "Can I show you the house I might buy? It's right around the corner from here. I'd love your opinion."

"Sure," Jack says.

"Turn here!" I direct. Jack hits the brakes hard and we round the corner. "And here!" Another sharp turn. We are laughing. "Nice stunt driving!"

"Good directions!"

"This white house here, with the red door." Jack screeches into the driveway. "The original part of the house is from the mid-1800s," I say. "It has lots of character, and there's also an addition in the back. It's got a new kitchen, the bathrooms are updated, and it has a nice back yard. What do you think?"

Jack cranes his neck to see the neighborhood and surrounding homes. "Good location. You've got other more expensive homes on the street. And it should be an easy walk to town."

"That's what I was thinking, too. I just walked into that house and liked it immediately. In about the first two minutes. My only hesitation—"

Jack is kissing me. His mouth is on mine, and at first, I am stunned, but then I am kissing him back, a little hesitantly at first but then hungrily. He is running his hands through my hair and then it becomes just full-on making out. I am kissing his neck, he is kissing mine. I kiss his mouth, behind his ears, I am feeling his shoulders, his chest, his hands are feeling mine. We are making out in the driveway of the house that I'm thinking of buying. This is some due diligence.

I pull back and catch my breath, staring at him. "Wow." He looks at me with those blue eyes and we smile a little shyly at each other. I reach out and smooth down some of his hair I've ruffled. "Have to put you back together," I say.

"Ready for dinner?" he says.

"Yes." And now we are proper again. I check my makeup and we drive the last mile to the restaurant in silence as though what just happened never did.

When we arrive, the maître d' greets Jack like an old friend and immediately leads us to what is probably the best table in the house. A rounded booth, cozy and private, set for two. It seems as though Jack has called ahead, or could it be that he's been here before?

We settle in and Jack drapes his arm around my shoulders. My head rests on his chest as we read one menu together.

He orders a very good bottle of red, and we get salads and steaks with peppercorn sauce. Between courses he kisses me. Passionately. We are all over each other and in the moment, neither one of us cares who sees, who watches. We're in our own little world.

♥

"Nightcap?" Jack says as we're driving back to his hotel.

"Sure." I can't imagine saying goodbye to him just yet.

He parks the car and begins leading me toward the back entrance. I stop and laugh. "Hey! This isn't the way to the bar," I say, yanking his arm in the opposite direction. He stands his ground. I twirl into him as though we are dancing. "The *other* side of the building."

He dips me backward and then I straighten up, laughing. "I just need to drop my jacket in the room," he says.

I follow behind, stand at the threshold, leaning on the door as he takes off his jacket and drapes it on the back of a chair.

"Why don't you come in?" he says. "I need to send a quick email."

Just one minute. I've heard that before. The door falls closed behind me, but I stay put, watching from a distance.

Jack sits down at the desk, slips on a pair of reading glasses, and types slowly and deliberately with two index fingers. *Cute.* Then he pulls off the glasses and closes the laptop. "You don't need to stand way over there by yourself," Jack says, coming toward me with a smile.

"It's . . . nice over here," I say, and then I crack up at how ridiculous that sounds. Jack cups my face and kisses me hard. He takes my hands from behind my back and intertwines our fingers, pinning my arms against the wall. "I thought we were having a drink," I murmur as he kisses my neck.

"We can have a drink," he whispers in my ear.

Suddenly I am in the air, in his arms, as if I'm weightless, and we're laughing. He carries me to the bed, laying me down in a way that's somewhere between careful and rough.

"What are you doing?"

"What would you like me to do?"

I pull him on top of me. "What . . . I would like . . . Mr. Carver . . ." I say, in staccato, punctuating each word with a kiss, ". . . is a drink."

"Alright." He slowly gets up and walks over to the mini bar. I smooth my hair and straighten my dress back down in the direction of my knees. "All types of drinks here," Jack says. "And look—here's a bottle of wine. Shall I open it?"

"We're not going to the bar?"

"Now why would we go to the bar when we have a perfectly good bottle of wine right here?"

"You—"

"Yes?"

"Are very tricky," I say. I am part amused, part frustrated by my own stupidity for falling for this trick.

Jack walks back to bed with two glasses of red wine. Then we are kissing again, the wine has already been pushed away, forgotten on the nightstand.

He's unzipping my dress. It's halfway down my spine. His hand is inside my dress, feeling my back, my shoulder, and for a moment, I wonder if he can feel it. The hollow where they scraped away the tumor that was eating my bones. My battle scar. I don't care. I want him to know all of me.

Black bra, black panties, his blue boxers. We are here, with little else. He looks at me laid out on the bed and says, "You are exquisite."

To feel desired. To feel my own. I struggle with what to say next, afraid to ruin this moment. But if I don't say it now, I know where this will go. "Do you have a condom?"

"I don't," Jack answers, as though he might find the question irrelevant.

"Then we can't," I say. "But we can do other things."

And we do. And it is a spectacular night.

♥

Where do I need to be? Wait. Evie is with her father. Everything is okay.

I drop my head back down into the pillow, staring at the outline of Jack's long back. Our bodies do not touch. I want to feel close to him again, this man in the bed, but does he even want me near? We're almost strangers. *How does Luke do this?*

I inch a little closer and rest the palm of my hand on his back and drift off to sleep again. He remains perfectly still.

It's later now, and Jack is sitting up in bed reading his phone.

"Good morning," I say, and before he can answer, I quickly scoot off to the bathroom and close the door. I look in the mirror. It ain't pretty. Last night's makeup smeared in every direction—swaths of red and black in the wrong places on my face. My hair looks crazy. I look like I've been doing exactly what I've been doing.

For the first time in many hours, I check my phone. There are two texts from Evan that came in the night before:

> **7:45 p.m.** Can I call you later?
> **9:36 p.m.** I will take that as a no.

Am I reading the tone correctly, or does he sound a little agitated? Or is that my own guilt talking and the circumstances of this morning? This particular morning. *My head hurts.*

I do the best I can to fix myself up. I borrow Jack's hard-bristled toothbrush and toothpaste that I find in the beat-up Ziploc bag on the counter and brush my teeth and return to bed. *This guy is a CEO. He can't spring for a toiletry bag?* It's kind of funny.

♥

I drive slowly back to my house. This will be a survival day. I feel stunned, off-balance.

Jack and I have said goodbye. We've had the awkward moment at the door of his hotel room, me back in last night's dress, my black wrap swaddled around me like a security blanket. We have said goodbye, and as I drive home, I recall he's said nothing about seeing me again. *You wanted this, Holly.*

I make myself strong coffee and toast.

I text Evan, who I now remember is flying to Ohio today to see Mella.

Me: Good morning. Sorry I was offline . . . safe flight today.
Evan: No worries. Everything okay with you?
Me: All good here. What time is your flight?
Evan: 1:45 p.m. Talk now?

He calls and asks when we can get together again, but as we go back and forth on days, we realize that scheduling is tricky. Our weekends with the children don't match up, so we decide to try again once he's back from Ohio.

The rest of the afternoon, I keep watching my phone, feeling nauseous, and it's not just my hangover and fatigue. Will I hear from him? I keep reminding myself that I didn't do anything I didn't want to do, so why do I feel so vulnerable?

I settle onto the couch with some tea and a stack of dating books, hoping insight might offer comfort.

The Rules ladies say to wait before sleeping with a guy. No surprise. Their advice is that the longer you wait, the longer the man has a chance to fall in love with who you really are, not just your body, and he'll have an opportunity to court you. This makes sense. And something else: "When you do decide you want to sleep with a guy, first ask yourself if you truly believe he will call or text you after ward." The fact that I am sitting here holding my breath, wondering if I'll ever hear from Jack again, means that I did sleep with him too soon.

And another book: *Why Men Love Bitches: From Doormat to Dreamgirl—A Woman's Guide to Holding Her Own in a Relationship* by Sherry Argov. Bitchwoman says, "Before sex, a man isn't thinking clearly and a woman is thinking clearly. After sex, it reverses. The man is thinking clearly and the woman isn't."

And then the advice of the "professional dominant," Ms. Arden Leigh, in *The New Rules of Attraction*. She doesn't speak of men, she speaks of "targets." While she doesn't buy into the same level of female passivity as *The Rules* ladies, Leigh does say that the target "must demonstrate that their interest in you encompasses far more than merely sex. Until you receive the appropriate signs from them, hold out on giving up the final prize." And she goes on to say that appropriate signs can vary from target to target, but he needs to be paying attention to you as a "whole person." That he goes out of his way to understand what you're really about.

Sometime just before 5:00 p.m., I hear my phone. A text has come in from Jack. The amount of relief I feel is almost embarrassing.

♥

CHAPTER 8

You Know Right Away

Another day househunting with my realtor. "This went on the market yesterday," she says, unlocking the door to a three-bedroom townhouse.

In the front hallway, there's a graciously curving dark wood staircase leading to a second level. To the right is a sitting room with high ceilings, a Venetian chandelier, and fireplace, and to the left, a large kitchen with plenty of light and windows overlooking beautifully landscaped grounds. There are hardwood floors throughout and five fireplaces in total.

"Wow. I love it," I say, just after a minute. "It's beautiful . . . the light, the layout . . ." I wander from room to room, picturing Evie and me here. The house is not too large and not too small. Elegant, yet homey.

"The garden outside the front door comes with the house!" the realtor calls. I peek out the window. There's a patio with a table and chairs, surrounded by flowers. A place to have a barbeque.

Later that morning, we view a few more homes, but I cannot get the first one out of my head. Nothing compares. "Let's go back to your office and put an offer together," I say, my heart thumping at the surety in my voice. *This is right. Do not second-guess yourself.*

The realtor and I work the numbers, and she promises to put in my offer immediately.

Later that night, I receive her text. "You got it!" it says.

"I got it?" I ask.

"Yes!" she confirms.

I'm elated. Who can I tell? Jack! He loves real estate. I text the news and just then my phone rings. "Congratulations!" Jack says. "Well done."

After we hang up, I bask in the good feelings, glancing around the kitchen of the house in the woods. Soon Evie and I will escape this place and the bad memories. Our new life is really starting.

My phone rings and it's my realtor again. "I'm so excited!" I say, not even bothering to say hello.

"Oh, Holly, there's been a miscommunication," she says, sighing. "Now the sellers are thinking that they want more money and to entertain more offers.

"What?"

"They are looking for a higher offer now and would like to entertain other offers for another ten days."

"Ten days? This isn't a miscommunication—"

"I think it's because the house has been on the market less than twenty-four hours and you made an offer right away. It's the psychology of the deal."

"Let me think about this," I say, hanging up.

My next call is back to Jack. "That's brokers, for you," he says, grunting, after I tell him that the seller of the house is a broker herself. There are three brokers in the mix. "What you do is say your offer is good for twenty-four hours, and if not, you'll move on." We talk through the pros and cons of the plan. "How badly do you want the house?" he asks.

"I really want it, I love it. But I also don't want to wait forever."

"Then give them a deadline."

I call the realtor and do exactly as Jack suggests. They get their closing date and other terms, but my price is firm. And they have twenty-four hours to give me their decision.

I go to bed that night feeling good about everything. If it's meant to be, it will somehow work out.

♥

Date #15: Which Came First, the Flip-Flops or the Foot Fungus?

Midmorning coffee date with Dylan, a six-foot-six, work-from-home single dad wearing a lumberjack shirt and flip-flops on a rainy day. Thick, yellowed toenails like a cheese rind.

Spends a lot of time talking about a female friend's rectal cancer. Dylan talks so much about cancer—this friend, then his cousin who carries a gene that pretty much guarantees an early demise—that I finally say, "Please no more cancer talk? It's depressing."

Dylan apologizes. He's actually a nice guy, just not the one for me.

I excuse myself and go to the ladies' room to check my phone. Two voice mail messages and a text from my realtor. They've accepted my offer and want to schedule the inspection for the weekend. And I need to get moving on selecting a real estate attorney. *Can this really be true?* I've got to hand it to Jack—he gives great advice.

Back at the table, Dylan tells me about his German ex-girlfriend who's in town, who will crash on his couch tonight. "She's going to want to fuck me," he says.

"Fuck you, huh? What will you do?" I ask.

He shrugs and laughs. "Nah," he answers.

Nah. I'm thinking the same thing.

♥

Date #16: Perfect Storm

Steve's online photo hair is like a young John Travolta's; in real life, it's gray and almost gone. He's is a ballroom-dancer-turned-TV-writer for an eighties hit TV show, turned Silicon Valley executive who adopted his former ballroom dance partner's child after she was sent to jail. She'd been an exotic dancer, but he swears they were just friends.

He's an accomplished sailor. His longest trip was more than three thousand miles solo to the Marquesa Islands in French Polynesia after his sister, his only sibling, committed suicide. No surprise, somewhere out on the open ocean in the middle of nowhere, he hit a major storm. For hours he fought but was overcome with exhaustion and went down below to sleep, knowing he may never wake up again. "Everyone at some point in their life has to decide whether they are going to live or die," he says.

He married and eventually divorced. He and the ex-wife remain friends, and she became a Buddhist priest. "That whole Buddhist concept of non-attachment is total bullshit," he says, which makes me laugh.

I don't know. He's certainly interesting and smart. He tells a good story, he's good company, but he's no Jack.

♥

Date #17: Fondly and Very Sincerely

It's a dark and stormy night as the cliché goes, and I'm just home from my first date with investment banker Thom when a text arrives from Luke:

Luke: OMG! How was the date?!?!
Me: Dude was 6'6". Cute, smart.

Luke: Did it hurt?

Me: It was a 1st date. C'mon!

Alas, the dude had baggage.

Luke: You'd never make it in the gay world, man ;-)

Baggage?

Me: Ex-wife who'd wake him at 1:00 a.m. and scream about everything he'd done wrong. Like how he arranged the knives and forks in the dishwasher. YOU MUST LOAD BY TYPE OF FORK! Sounds like Gitmo.

Luke: Hate her already.

Me: And they have twins to raise together.

Luke: Don't envy him.

Me: Poor Thom. I've never had to look up so high to get a good night kiss. In the rain. As he held an umbrella over us.

Luke: Very sweet!

Me: It WAS.

Two days after our date, Thom sends a text about as long as his femur:

Hi Holly:

I really enjoyed our date. When I contacted you, I thought we were likely a good match for one another, and our dinner confirmed it (for me at least). You are very attractive, intelligent, easy to talk to, and of course—tall! And we're geographically well matched, too.

However, I thought about it pretty long before I contacted you because I've been seeing someone for a few weeks. Early stages. You seemed like such a good fit, I went for it nonetheless because I thought if I let the opportunity pass, I might never have the chance to meet you. Again, you're the only person I've contacted after 8 months of 24 profiles being sent to me daily (that's the top 0.4%, just so ya know) . . .

You said at dinner that all relationships are heading somewhere—words of wisdom that I hadn't really contemplated before, but with which I totally agree. I think a lot of guys would likely try to juggle multiple relationships simultaneously to "see where they go." However, for me, I'm a little old-fashioned in that regard, and it's just not my style. It doesn't seem fair to the people I'd be dating and it has the potential for bad endings—not to mention that it sounds really complicated!

For me, our meeting is a case of a great potential match but bad timing.

Who knows where the relationship I've started may lead (per your wisdom above) but I'm really glad I met you and there's a very high likelihood I will be contacting you again in the future when the timing is better for me. I know that I am running a great risk that when I do, your timing may be bad (I'm sure your inbox is alive with active suitors) or perhaps this is all moot because you didn't feel as connected with me as I did with you. But again, I'm an old-fashioned, one-girl-at-a-time man.

I'd love to know your thoughts on this.

Fondly, and very sincerely,

Thom

Sweet Thom, so honest and upfront. I answer that a phone conversation makes sense. And right away Thom calls and we talk and it's a good conversation. He's just frank and says that he likes the woman he's currently dating a lot, and while they're not exclusive, he wants to just focus on her. He doesn't add anything new to the discussion, but I don't regret taking it through. I thank him for his candor and won't hear from him again. He's right. Our timing is off, and isn't so much of life and dating about just that? Luck and timing. Two people wanting the same things at the same time. Throw in big chemistry and then *bam!*

And now Thom has got me wondering, too, if I, like him, should just focus on one special person at a time?

Joan and the dating books would say heck no to that. Love is a war, and you have to fight on as many fronts as you can manage, all at the same time. Because time is of the essence, especially by middle age.

Whatever the metaphor—war, or perhaps a marathon—I know I have to keep fighting. I just have to keep going.

♥

CHAPTER 9

Busy is a Load of You-Know-What

Meanwhile, on the Jack front, I'm becoming more and more frustrated. He says he's going to get "organized," that's he's just been so busy, and we'll get together, but it hasn't happened. It's been weeks since our last date, yet he texts regularly. Are we just pen pals?

I've picked up another dating book for the stash: *He's Just Not That into You: The No-Excuses Truth to Understanding Guys* by Greg Behrendt and Liz Tuccillo.

Even though the book is cowritten by a woman, the voice of Greg dominates throughout. It's the voice of your brother or your one good, platonic guy friend who doesn't want to sleep with you, stating the honest, brutal truth about men. Sorry to break the bad news, sweetheart, but this is the way it is. On many dating topics, Greg and The Rules chicks are not far apart, and they completely agree on who does the asking:

> "Don't get tricked into asking him out. If he likes you, he'll do the asking. If you can find him, then he can find you. If he wants to find you, he will. Just because you like to lead doesn't mean he wants to dance. Some traditions are born of nature and last through time for a reason."

And Greg and *Rules* chicks agree again about reliability:

> "Here's something else to think about: calling when you say you're going to is the very first brick in the house you are building of love and trust. If he can't lay this one stupid brick down, you ain't never gonna have a house, baby, and it's cold outside."

And as I read some more, there are lines that really jump out at me:

> "Don't spend your time on and give your heart to any guy who makes you wonder about anything related to his feelings for you."

Okay, Jack. I still don't understand where he's coming from.

And then Greg's coup de grace:

> "I'm about to make a wild, extreme, and severe relationship rule: THE WORD 'BUSY' IS A LOAD OF CRAP AND IS MOST OFTEN USED BY ASSHOLES. The word 'busy' is the relationship Weapon of Mass Destruction. Remember: Men are never too busy to get what they want. If a guy truly likes you, but for personal reasons he needs to take things slow, he will let you know that immediately. He won't keep you guessing, because he'll want to make sure you don't get frustrated and go away."

Greg is crystal clear. Things don't bode well for me and Mr. Carver.

♥

It's already May, and I run that first half-marathon in a week. I'm nervous. What if I fail?

Sunday morning, I awake alone. Evie is with David for the weekend and the house is quiet. I sit in the kitchen in an arm chair, my slippered feet propped on the ottoman, staring out toward the black ridge of trees against the brightening orange sky, drinking coffee.

I've had tons of sleep. I stayed in last night and thought and felt and dwelled with some difficult feelings. Reveled in some good ones, too. Realized that sometimes I need to just sit with the feelings of loneliness and loss. Just let it all be felt. There are no shortcuts through grief.

I think about Jack. Do I just love bastards the way men love bitches? Not that he's necessarily a bastard; it's more of the edge of his air of mystery . . . and maybe that he's ultimately unattainable?

It seems that I'm drawn to men with complications—guys like Zach. I realize that women who are drawn to broken men are really looking for a project. To "fix" them. Yet I know you cannot fix anyone—only yourself. Zach was young, wild, a little directionless, exciting. The antithesis of David. He kept me on my toes and loved me passionately but was ultimately fickle. Still, letting go has been excruciating, and I know he's struggling, too. Zach leaves messages on my phone: "Meet me Thursday night at seven," he says, pleading to have dinner at our favorite restaurant. It's so hard to turn your back on someone you love.

The time before the dinner request, Zach had called to say that he was deleting me from his phone. That if I want to get in touch, I will have to contact him. Push and pull, push and pull.

These days when I get texts from him, my forehead grows tight, my breath shortens. Sometimes he saddens me, in other moments, I'm agitated and angry and I can observe that in myself now. All of the running, yoga, and meditation is teaching me to listen to my body and tune in to read the signs. I can see the impact of stress. More than ever, I know Zach is the wrong man for me, and I need to let go. I don't answer Zach's phone calls or texts and hope the silence speaks for itself.

♥

Date #18: Blinded by The White

This will be my fourth date with Evan. Feeling some pressure. Can't say that I haven't been warned.

The plan is to have dinner together in New York and then a nightcap at his apartment afterward.

I'll be going to his apartment—Ms. Slow-on-the-Uptake actually knows what this implies now. There's going to be a kiss or two at least. Maybe a close up of the eye.

I drive in and park at a garage near Evan's apartment. I'm wearing jeans, a white silk top, a leather jacket, and heels.

I cab over to the Village where we have dinner at Lupa. We drink a hearty red wine, eat perfect pasta, and have an all-around good time. There is only one uncomfortable moment when Evan is talking about Jane and refers to her as his "wife." He sees my expression change. "Soon-to-be-ex-wife," he quickly corrects. But it's out there again. He is still married.

We head over to his place. On the way, he puts his hand on my knee and gives me a deep kiss. I'm feeling tentative, but the wine and his touch helps me unwind a little.

Inside his apartment, my first impression is that there's a hell of a lot of white. White everywhere. There's a white sofa and a few pictures, unhung, propped up against very white walls. *Blinding white: The official color of divorce.* "This is all I got," Evan says, motioning dramatically into the Spartan space. There is a bitterness to his proclamation, and once again, the ugliness of an unresolved divorce hangs in the air.

I tell him his apartment has promise: it's downtown and has a good view of the water. The sky is fading from pink into black, and the lights of New Jersey twinkle in the distance. "You just need a little time to make it home," I say. "Maybe hang some of these pictures?" I say, picking up a black and white print of the Brooklyn Bridge.

"I have to give you the full tour. It'll take all of two seconds," Evan says, grabbing my hand, leading toward the bedroom.

Inside, the window is bare, and the light from the city filters in. He has a king-sized bed with a white duvet, two plain pillows, and nothing else. "Wait here," Evan says and heads into the bathroom, closing the door behind him. *What is he doing?* I sit down on the edge of the bed in the dimly lit room, glancing between the glaring light of the hallway and the soft city view outside.

Then Evan appears in the doorway, his profile silhouetted against the bright light. He has stripped down to boxer shorts, and the image is like that of a giant man-child, baby Buddha, his belly slightly distended. "I've brought some baby oil," he says seductively.

"Baby oil?"

"Will you rub it on me?" he asks, falling slowly, like a giant sequoia, onto the bed.

"Uhh . . . okay," I say.

"My back is a little sore," he says, passing me the bottle.

"Sorry to hear it."

This is some weird foreplay.

He removes his glasses and stretches out on the bed, spread-eagled. I flip open the pink lid and reluctantly rub some oil into my hands. *Why exactly am I doing this?* The smell of the baby oil nearly sickens me. Anyone who has ever diapered a baby likely associates it with childhood and Pampers. I feel like I'm in a nursery, about to read a story before naptime for baby.

His skin is warm and unusually soft, his body a little doughy. "Ahhh . . ." he murmurs.

Half-heartedly, I rub his back for a few minutes, and before this goes any further, I say, "I really should go." I dart to the bathroom and wash the oil off my hands. *Yuck.*

"That was a nice time," Evan says as he walks me to the garage where my car is parked. As we wait for the attendant to get my car, Evan sees me pull out four singles from my wallet. "Oh, don't tip him that much," he says sharply.

"It's okay," I answer. "I want to."

Evan frowns and shrugs.

Why can't I tip a hardworking man?

I get into my car, and he leans in and gives me a kiss through the open window. "Text me when you get home," he says.

♥

My first thought this morning is that I need to tell Evan we can't date anymore. This doesn't feel right. *The baby oil!* I call him. "Can you talk?" I say.

"I'm at the club about to tee off with my father, but I can for a minute."

I clear my throat. "Ugh, no easy way to say this. I don't think we should date anymore."

"Really?" Evan pauses. "Really?"

"Yeah. I'm sorry."

"I mean . . . I respect your decision, but . . ."

"It's hard for me to say this. But one of the things that's really bothering me is that you're still married." *Bad enough without the baby oil.*

"You know my wife and I are almost over."

"I just feel that we are overweight in baggage."

Evan starts to laugh. "I like that. Like an airline!"

"Exactly . . ."

"No one ever breaks up with me," Evan says. "Can you do me a favor? I'd really appreciate it." His tone has softened. "Can we talk about this in person? Will you at least give me that?"

"Well . . ."

"Thanks. Gotta go—my dad is here."

And he hangs up saying that we'll get together soon and I am kicking myself, thinking that damn it, this is like that old *Seinfeld* episode where George tries to break up with his girlfriend but she won't grant her permission so they're still together. I suck at this.

Two hours later, my doorbell rings. I open the door and a delivery man is standing there with an enormous vase of flowers. I tear open the envelope:

> Holly,
> We can make it to "carry-on."
> I'm not giving up on you.
> Love,
> Evan

Points for wit and persistence.

Later in the day, Jack calls me from the airport in Boston, en route to San Diego. Well, Jack had texted me the night before, saying that he would call, and he did. *(Hear that, Greg?)* It's something.

He asks how Evie is doing. "Better," I answer. "She's getting used to the idea of moving. Changing schools, potentially."

"And you introducing her to men thirteen years your junior?"

"Six! Very funny." I had told him about Zach the first night we met.

And we go back and forth and rib each other and I wish him a safe flight and we hang up.

A few minutes later, I text him: "I forgot to ask you something." I know he's boarded the plane. I figure he'll get my message when he lands.

But then my phone rings. *Shit! It's him!* I stare at the bouncing phone, afraid to pick up. "Hello?" My heart is pounding.

"Well, I couldn't leave that hanging out there."

"Um, I forgot to ask you what you want for your birthday."

"Oh!" He laughs nervously. "It's something you're going to have to deliver in person."

"What do you have in mind . . .?"

"Birthday wishes only come true if you keep them a secret . . ."

"Oh, really?" I pause. *I don't care what the damn books say.* "I miss you," I say. My heart pounds faster.

"Me too." Jack laughs nervously. "No, I don't miss myself! I mean I miss you, too."

"Have a safe flight."

I stare at my phone and grin like an idiot. Sweet awkwardness. The first thing resembling tenderness.

♥

Date #19: Your Treat

Staring at Evan's bouquet of flowers on my dining room table, I think maybe I should give him one last chance. Don't I want to be absolutely sure one way or another? It's Sunday, early afternoon. "Dinner in CT tonight?" I text.

My phone rings. "Only if you buy," Evan says.

"Deal." We make arrangements for Evan's train from Grand Central and that I'll pick him up from the station. *"Only if you buy?" Am I making a mistake here?*

But I've been thinking about seeing Evan again because he seems to genuinely care for me. He can be funny, is emotionally available, and really wants a relationship.

Don't I owe that a chance? Hell, compared to Jack, Evan has a lot going for him. There's little guesswork about his feelings for me, and that's a good sign. Maybe the baby oil incident was . . . just a false start? Sometimes it takes time to figure out the physical, and we get along pretty well otherwise.

When I pick up Evan from the station, I watch him descending the stairs. He's striking in a button-down shirt with a navy sweater thrown over his shoulders, looking right at home in Connecticut. I drive us to the restaurant, a casual seafood place with a view of Long Island Sound.

"Thanks for making the trek out here," I say.

He looks happy. "Thanks for suggesting it." He orders a beer, and as he drinks, I try not to stare at the foam on his upper lip or his glass eye that catches the sunlight streaming in the window. Evan updates me on his divorce with Jane. "The California house. She wants half of it."

"Oh."

"And that's unfair. I put a lot more money into it," he says, his voice taking on an edge. *Is this about money or flexibility and generosity?*

"I guess your lawyer will advise you on the best position to take?" I say. And Evan answers that this is about fairness, and it's plain wrong how Jane approaches everything and the lawyer will do as Evan tells him.

"Aren't you in California soon?" I say, tying to snap him out of this mood.

"Good memory! For my niece's christening."

"Will your parents go, too?"

"Yeah—my dad, my mom, brothers, everyone." Evan tilts his head and smiles. "My mom is going to love you!"

I'm a deer in headlights. "You think so?"

When the check comes, I pay, as promised, and he thanks me with a wink and I know I'm never going to meet his mother. I don't want to meet his mother. Evan is not someone I'm ever going to love passionately. How much more information did I need? Didn't I know it even before I picked him up at the train station?

When I drop him at the station, I'm a coward, even as he says, "Next weekend is your race! You're going to do great," and he throws his arms around me and my heart sinks and I don't have the guts nor the energy to tell him we're done. I don't want a scene or debate; I just want him on the train. "Let's talk this week," Evan says, and I agree. I know better, but I promise myself I'll break things off soon, after my race.

♥

It's hard to really get to know someone if you rarely spend time together. Some people enjoy virtual relationships of daily texting, the random phone call, the occasional hook up, but not me. I'm beginning to wonder if this loose arrangement is what Jack is actually seeking.

I'm wondering, too, if there may be parallels between dating and real estate, at least from a psychological standpoint. Deadlines to clarify thinking and make a call one way or another. Are we in or out? Don't you know almost instantly when a home feels right? Our instincts about people are similar, aren't they?

Last week, Jack called on Tuesday—twice. We texted a lot on Wednesday and Thursday. He called me on Thursday, his birthday. Friday, he seemed detached—just a few texts. Mine was the last. Then nothing. Saturday, nothing. Sunday, zero. The Monday afternoon after Jack goes to San Diego, I receive a text:

> "I survived the weekend. Kept running into glasses containing vodka! How was yours?"

Who was he drinking with in San Diego? Was he really at an economic conference? This dating shit can be exhausting.

By Tuesday, it's all really bothering me. I still don't have a read on Jack. What is the point of all the texts, the phone conversations, if it doesn't go anywhere? Where I keep getting my hopes up, only to be disappointed. I don't want a pen pal; I want a boyfriend.

So do I want to try to push this toward clarity? I guess I do. I fear I'm just his booty call and ego boost. I have zero interest in that role. I fear I'm already feeling too much for him, that it's not reciprocal and I'm going to get hurt.

Tuesday morning, I get out of the shower and wipe the fog off the bathroom mirror. I see the furrows across my forehead, the preoccupied look in my eyes. This is eating at me and enough is enough. I pick up my phone and send Jack a text: "Why are we staying in touch?" My heart begins to race. Maybe this will start the conversation.

He replies immediately. *"Read" receipts are one tiny gift in dating a sixty-something.* "I don't know. Because we want to?" And then the Jack-style ducking and dodging begins.

"Maybe the fact that we haven't talked about it speaks for itself?" I write.

More vague answers.

But I keep going. I'm the pissed-off chick on a relationship status quest. "Every relationship is going somewhere. It seems we're more on a path to friendship? Even though I like you more than a friend," I say. *Should I be texting this? Probably not. And you sound like a high school kid. This is a dumb way to approach a serious topic.* "I'm sorry. I shouldn't address this via text," I write, finally.

"Agreed," Jack says. I stop. No more texts. Everything is now hanging in the air, awkward and unresolved. The rest of the day, I inwardly cringe and there's not another word from him.

You took action on something that was important to you. If he really cared, he'd pick up the phone and not leave you twisting.

Nothing more Tuesday. Nothing on Wednesday or Thursday.

It's over. I won't hear from him again. At least I know where I stand.

I tell myself that all I can do is learn from the experience, but deep down I'm raw. I got intimate too soon with Jack, before I knew whether or not he cared for me. It's painful, but there's nothing to be done about it now. Lesson learned.

♥

CHAPTER 10

Walk, Don't Run, Run, Don't Stop

It's Memorial Day weekend and my race.

My wiseass friends are behind me. Rose sends an e-card that says "I'll be half cheering for you during your half-marathon. Good luck!"

Luke is on board to be with Evie for the roughly two hours it will take me to complete the race, along with friends Ralph and Bradford, who will also cheer from the sidelines.

Evie gets out of school at noon and we set off, driving north through Connecticut, into the Berkshires of western Massachusetts.

As I drive, I remember the visits up here to see Zach when we were very much in love, each mile bringing me closer to him. My memories wash with the landscape and the four seasons that we were together. We began in the fall in Indian summer, when the ripe colors of autumn bannered across the rolling hills and mountains. Then it was winter, the black starkness of the bare trees, where we'd spend half the weekend in bed or by the fire, reading, listening to music, watching the snow fall. Sometimes Zach would play his guitar and sing to me, his voice low and soft, his long hair falling across one eye. Then after a month of rain and mud, there was spring's gentle green and walks in the woods before the heat of summer set in. I'm returning to a place of memories and where this man still lives.

The race. Can I pull this off? My goal is just to run and not stop until I cross the finish line after 13.1 miles. We don't stop. That's what I've told myself countless times as I've trained over five months, in spite of the fatigue, blisters, aches, and boredom.

Zach taught me how to run. He said that almost always there is something to overcome. Maybe it will be a twinge in your knee or a runny nose or stiff hip or challenging weather. It's rare that things are perfect, so when the irritant inevitably comes, he said to just acknowledge it. "Say to yourself, *there it is*, and keep going."

Running this race, here, on Zach's turf, in spite of our split, feels like a small victory, an overcoming of sorts. I want to show Evie that when you set out to do something, you see it through till the end. You don't hide. Yet I must admit, I'm afraid, still, worried we might bump into him, and what would that mean for her?

Jack is on my mind, too. There's the sad resignation that I'll probably never hear from him again. He's incommunicado since the texting incident. I'm hopeless.

It's early evening when Evie and I check into the inn. The innkeeper, Craig, whom I know from previous stays, pours some wine, and we stand on his sweeping lawn that's framed by forest, catching up after a few months, watching Evie play with Craig's golden retriever, Daisy. Daisy and Evie are in heaven, rolling in the grass and running and playing fetch. They wander into the woods. "Daisy needs a better stick!" Evie calls as she traipses through the trees, snapping off branches.

Craig and I are chatting about my race on Sunday, when out of the corner of my eye, I see a dark shadow in the woods. Suddenly it comes into focus. *My God, that's a bear.* A large black bear is about fifty feet away from Evie and the dog. "Look!" I say, ready to sprint for my daughter, but Craig grabs my arm.

"Do not run," Craig whispers. "Evie!" Craig calls in a low tone. She looks up, branches in her hand. She has not yet seen the bear. I can tell by the look on her face that she senses the urgency in Craig's voice but doesn't understand why. "Evie, what I want you to do right now is slowly walk over to Daisy and hold her by the collar, okay?"

"Okay . . ." Evie says. She still doesn't know.

"Now. It's very important," Craig says. He turns to me. "You get Evie, I'll get Daisy," and we begin walking toward Evie and the dog. It takes everything in me to calmly walk and not run. The bear has stopped about twenty feet behind them. My heart feels like it's going to pound out of my chest. Evie still doesn't understand, and my eyes are riveted on her. Every step is an eternity. I must get my daughter, I must get my daughter. If that animal so much as touches her, I will fight it to the death with my bare hands, with everything I have.

I am almost to Evie and then she looks over her shoulder, sees the bear, and wets her pants. "It's okay, sweetie," I whisper, taking her hand. "It's okay. Let's go. Walk, don't run."

Craig has grabbed Daisy and the four of us are now together, slowly moving away from the bear. Now my back is to it, something I will later realize I should never have done, but all I can think about is getting Evie out of there. We walk across the lawn that seems even more enormous now, and as we get closer to the inn, we begin to move faster and faster, now nearly to a run as we near a basement entrance. "This way!" Craig says, throwing open a door. We dash in and he bolts it behind us.

"Oh my God!" I say. "A bear?"

"Mommy . . .?" Evie is crying, and I wrap my arms around her.

Craig picks up the phone and dials 911.

♥

A short time later, Evie and I sit outside on the inn's patio, having dinner. Neither one of us are eating much, we are both still too upset, coming off adrenalin and sickening fear. I drink wine, trying to calm my nerves, looking out to the dark woods where the bear was. It's gone.

"It's funny," I say to Evie, rubbing her back, "I thought I'd taught you everything you needed to know about how to be safe . . . how to look both ways before crossing a street, stranger danger, water safety, but bears? It never even occurred to me."

"You're right, Mom," she says, and we shake our heads and laugh a little.

I pick up my phone and see that Evan has texted. It's a thoughtful message, asking if I've arrived safely, and my spirits sink further. This is a guy who cares for me, and I'm going to disappoint him in about forty-eight hours when I break things off. I just don't want any more drama before my race. I text him about the bear.

"So scary," Evan writes. "I don't know what to say other than I wish I could hold you."

Hold me?

The ringing of my phone interrupts. *Wait. It's Jack?*

"I'm sorry for being muddled," Jack blurts out as I'm still in disbelief that it's him on the other end. And he goes on to say that his sister has been visiting from San Francisco. "All week she's been telling me that I've been making all the wrong decisions. She says I need to pick up the phone and call you."

"I'm really glad you did." I'm still stunned, and then I tell him the bear story.

Later, Jack and I will text and I will apologize for being muddled when he called.

"Because your firstborn was almost eaten by a bear? Understandable," he says, along with emoticons of a bear, a baby, and a terrified face. This makes me laugh. And I realize I want a man who will make me laugh when the bear comes out of the woods. Laugh with me, just keep me laughing.

That night as I try to fall asleep, my head swirls with the events of the day. I keep seeing the dark shadow in the woods threatening my little girl. Sometimes our instincts are off. Our survival is honed through learned skills; we cannot always rely on instinct. You learn to walk, don't run. And I see, too, how ironically it's the things that we never even imagined, never even occurred to us to worry about—maybe the sanity of the people we have long loved or lumps in the body that practically grow overnight—that might truly threaten us. So, isn't worry pointless? You just need the faith that you can handle whatever it is when it comes, out of the blue, out of nowhere, out of the woods.

♥

The day of my race dawns sunny and cool. Ideal running weather.

I drink coffee and choke down a couple of bananas and whole wheat bread with peanut butter and a ton of water. I'm just a bundle of nerves. I lay on the floor and stretch a while and then try meditating for a few minutes, focusing on a good outcome. *Run and don't stop, that's all you have to do.*

By 7:30 a.m., Luke, Evie, and I meet up at a local park where the race begins. Evie is thrilled to get Luke to herself for a couple of hours. Luke says that they will have breakfast before heading to the halfway point to cheer me on. I hand Luke my car keys and my phone. "You can do it, Mom," Evie says, squeezing my hands. I kiss the top of her head.

Runners and spectators gather together to sing the national anthem, and I tear up a little as I sing, feeling deeply grateful just to be here, for my health, and all of the good things in my life. And then it's announced: *"On your mark . . .!"* and finally I'm off on my race, swept up in the crowd of runners, the sound of dozens of feet pounding the pavement, the collective excitement, the whoops and hollers, the nervous coughing and adjusting of earphones and fanny packs and water bottles. I look back to wave at Luke and Evie, who are whistling and cheering. I hope Evie remembers this day. I want her to know that we must always strengthen our bodies, minds, and spirits. We do not stop.

The first five miles determines the rest of the race. I remind myself to find my pace, to not be influenced by the other runners who may be sprinting ahead. It's only when you find your own sustainable rhythm for the long haul that you have a chance at finishing. And your pace must be balanced, too, with a small reserve for the final few miles, when you pour it on with everything you've got.

As I hit my stride, I check in with myself. My nerves have eased. *Here I am. I'm doing it.* I feel my body. Nothing hurts, everything feels limber and strong. And the weather is sunny and cool, I'm not too hot, I'm not too cold, I'm not hungry nor thirsty. Everything is perfect, which is totally unexpected. There it is. It's perfect.

Each mile, I feel strong, and I look up and enjoy the gorgeous spring views with the hills and lilacs and old farmhouses and the lakes, running past the very towns and scenery depicted in Norman Rockwell's paintings.

I think about Jack and the surprise call. I think about Evan and understanding, finally, that I shouldn't be lukewarm about anyone I date. And that I need to end things with Evan kindly but without excess apology because we cannot help how we feel.

I think about Zach possibly being at the finish line today, too. No matter what happens, I will handle it.

The first ten miles are a relative breeze, and then things begin to take a turn for the worse. Around mile ten, I begin to feel pain in my foot. It's a blister the size of a quarter, and with each step, it hurts more and more. *There it is.* The pain grows to agonizing, it slows me down, I swear I can feel it oozing through my sock, but I work through it and just keep going. How can I let a lousy blister ruin it for me now? This is mostly a mental game at this point. Zach said if you're fed and hydrated, your body can endure for a long time. The rest of it is just in your head. I dig in, trying to ignore my discomforts and that I'm completely bathed in sweat, from every hair on my head through to my blistered feet, which are slipping around inside my shoes.

And then, finally, the blessed banner for the finish line comes into view. The assembled crowds are cheering, and the name of each runner is announced over a loudspeaker as he or she finishes. More than anything I want to see Evie, especially Evie, I'm doing this for us.

The final stretch of the race is under a canopy of trees and the shade is welcome relief as I run the final yards, and then I see my girl. Just past the finish line, I run straight into Evie and Luke's arms and burst into tears. "Mommy," Evie says, clinging to me. I can't say anything, I'm just so tired, happy, grateful, relieved. Someone slips a cheap medal around my neck, but in that moment, it feels like the greatest thing ever.

"Eww, you need a shower," my friend Ralph quips. Ralph is the only gay Republican I know, and certainly the best dressed. I give him a big hug and make sure I rub a little extra sweat on him.

There is no Zach. All is calm.

"Let's go for lunch," Bradford, Ralph's partner, suggests and we all agree on where to meet up.

"I want to ride in your convertible!" Evie says to Ralph and Bradford.

"Sure," Ralph says. "You just have to tell me, what is your *least* favorite music?" he asks.

"Opera," Evie answers without hesitation.

As Ralph, Bradford, and Evie drive off in Ralph's red Mercedes, top down, Ralph blasts opera while Bradford laughs, giving the thumbs-up as Evie screeches in the back seat, hands covering her ears.

As I'm dressing for dinner, my phone rings.

"How did it go?" It's Jack, calling to ask about my race, congratulating me. "Now that your training is over, how will you spend your time?"

"I'm sure I'll find ways to amuse myself."

"How about a visit to Boston next weekend?"

"Boston?"

"There is a hotel near my townhouse. I can book you a room there. I wouldn't want to be presumptuous," Jack says.

When Jack and I wish each other a good night and hang up, I'm nothing short of elated. This has been an incredible day.

There's just one last bit of unfinished business. Evan. I grab my phone again and break things off with him, once and for all. He's unhappy, maybe even a little angry, but sometimes there's just no good way to deliver bad news. And the next morning, as Evie and I head back to Connecticut, I feel a deep swell of gratitude for my daughter and good friends and the lessons learned this weekend. Not to mention a growing excitement about my upcoming trip to Boston.

♥

CHAPTER 11

City on a Hill

Date #20: Rainbows & Matchmakers

There's a romance to the train, as though it's from another time, as if the journey alters time. Seeing the landscape transition, the dense city opening up to become fields with sparse trees and then marsh and quaint towns with churches and sea views. More space to think and adjust to the changes to come, being rocked back and forth by the train's steady rhythm, the whistle and whoosh like a lullaby as you barrel toward a new destination.

I'm going to Boston to see Jack. I've wanted this for what feels like a very long time. For him to let me in.

When I arrive, we will have dinner with another couple, Drew and Rachel. Drew lives in Boston, a divorced father of three, while Rachel is a single parent of one.

In some ways, meeting his friends feels a little sudden, yet flattering, too. It's a good sign, isn't it, when a man introduces you to his friends?

As the train pulls into South Station, the sun breaks through clouds and everything looks brighter. And standing at the end of the platform is Jack. My butterflies have returned. I stare down at my sandaled feet moving toward him and once again I have a hard time meeting his gaze. This man can make me feel shy as no one has before.

Then he wraps an arm around my shoulders and gives me a kiss on the mouth and unburdens me, taking the suitcase from my hand. I have to recognize him again— so elegant and weathered, like an old-time movie star.

As we drive, I glance around at the city that I haven't visited in five years, wondering. It was in this place that I was first diagnosed with my tumor. When I thought—and it was a real possibility based on what the doctors believed at that point—that I could be dead in a year. That tumor changed my marriage, me, it changed everything. It was the dress rehearsal on my mortality, the opening act to my divorce.

"I'll show you some of my favorite places," Jack says. He grew up here. Boston is home.

Jack and I have continued to dance around the sleeping arrangements, but I've held firm and said I will stay at the waterfront hotel a short distance from his townhouse. There's little downside, I figure, to having my own space, and who knows what may transpire this weekend. I'm still getting to know this man.

Jack checks me in to the hotel and we grin at each other in the elevator as we ride up to my room. "I was thinking that we could go out on my boat before dinner."

"I'd like that," I answer. "Let me quickly get changed."

He sits down in a chair in the corner, legs outstretched, arms folded behind his head, watching me dig through my suitcase for some warmer clothes. He just keeps smiling at me, like he's waiting for a show. "What?" I say.

"Nothing," he says, grinning.

As I walk past him, he gives me a swat on the rear end and I catch his wrist. "Keep your distance," I say, eyeing him and then the bed. "I know your tricks." I try to look stern, but it's difficult. He's so damn charming.

I step into the bathroom, closing the door behind me.

"No need to change in there," I hear him call, but there is. I'm still finding my bearings. Just a few days ago, I thought he'd disappeared for good.

We head down to Jack's dock. Jack boards first and then takes my hand, helps me aboard, and we're off.

The skies overhead look moody, with some dark gray clouds and a wind that hints of rain. As Jack confidently navigates the boat through the steel-blue water, he stands, and I sit in the white leather seat beside him, my hand resting on the back of his calf. It feels natural to touch him, so I do.

We bounce along the waves for a time, feeling the wind slap our faces, breathing in the thick salt air, the clouds above shifting dark-hued colors from grays and blues to black. The drizzle turns to a downpour and we head back to shore.

♥

Inside Jack's house with floor-to-ceiling water views from every window, he opens a bottle of wine. I compliment him on his Spanish-style dining room table and chairs, the focal point of the room. It stands in sharp contrast to his other with furniture, which is all modern. "My grandfather brought that back from Madrid a long time ago," he says.

"Looks almost too beautiful to use," I say, running my fingers over the delicate red velvet on the back of a chair.

"But we do. Last Thanksgiving, in fact," Jack says, handing me a glass of red. I wonder who was around this table last Thanksgiving. His former girlfriend of fourteen years, Nadia, presumably—another thought I try to push out of my head.

"Let me take you upstairs," Jack says. "I'm renovating, excuse the mess." As we wade through a disaster zone of plastic, tools, and a heavy film of white dust, he shows me the plan for what will be an office, a media room, guest room, and a new bathroom and laundry area.

"This is going to be gorgeous when it's finished," I say, picking up some of the tile samples he's selected for the bathroom. *Are the choices his? He said Nadia is an interior designer.*

"And then up here," Jack says, leading me up another level with more water views from every room and the tour abruptly dead-ends in his master bedroom.

"What a great house," I say as casually as I can, trying to pretend that we're not standing here in his bedroom. I will have to squeeze past him to get downstairs if I want to leave. But it's too late. Jack gives me a long, deep kiss and then picks me up and lays me down on the bed.

"Your favorite trick," I murmur. A few kisses later, it's abundantly clear that if I don't get myself out of this bed, right now, we will be here the rest of the night. "Let's go downstairs," I say, wrapping a blanket around me. Jack, shirtless, joins me, and we talk easily, savoring our wine. I watch him, smiling, admiring his brawny, fit, body. From his weightlifting, golf, and yoga, of all things. He seems the last man on the planet who'd be interested in yoga.

"Look," he says, pointing out the front window. A brilliant, perfect rainbow arches above the harbor.

♥

We walk to an Italian restaurant in the North End where Drew and Rachel are waiting for us.

Rachel is probably in her forties, with long brown hair and the slightest hint of a Long Island accent. She glows when she talks about her young son. Drew is a round-faced, sandy-haired Irish Catholic, born and bred in Boston. I like them both immediately.

We all agree that we need red wine and meatballs to start the dinner off right, and Rachel smiles at Drew and brushes his arm. They've been together seven years, and their ease with each other shows.

"How often do you see each other?" I ask.

"We take turns going back and forth between New York and Boston. About once a week," Rachel says.

"And vacations and holidays," Drew adds, putting his arm around Rachel. This seems reassuring, as though how they do it might bode well for Jack and me.

"Dating," Jack says with a sigh. "Every Christmas morning, I get a call from the same matchmaker," he says.

"Matchmaker?" Rachel says, startled.

"She's been trying to set me up for years. She calls me every Christmas morning and says, 'Are you alone again?' And every year I am."

No one speaks or looks at each other. Jack gives a low, nervous chuckle and changes the subject.

♥

Date #21: Every Happiness

Jack and I wake up together in my hotel room, mid-morning. So much for separate spaces. Then we wander, hand-in-hand, to his house so he can change his clothes.

Today we will spend breakfast, lunch, and dinner together. We will talk and walk everywhere, all over Boston, around the North End and the Waterfront, then Faneuil Hall and Boston Common.

We are getting ready to head out the door when he picks up his phone. "Text from Drew," he announces. "Rachel likes Holly and Rachel doesn't like anyone!" Jack reads aloud.

I laugh. "I like Rachel, too."

"Jury is out on her, though."

"Really?" I say.

Jack tells me that Drew is fragile—vulnerable, even, after his divorce. "His ex-wife cheated on him," Jack says. "He probably thinks he can't do better."

What's wrong with Rachel? I like her.

"Rachel is pushing for a commitment," Jack adds.

"He told you?"

"He's not ready for it."

"Hasn't Drew been divorced seven or eight *years*?"

"Sounds about right," Jack answers, putting on his sunglasses. "Shall we?" he says, beckoning to the door.

I'm puzzled by Jack's perspective. And over the weekend, in our many hours of conversation, this theme will emerge again—that women are trying to catch and reel in the men they are with. They push for the C word: commitment. Seemingly an evil thing; it's a cliché of commitment phobia.

Later, when Jack is showing me the first place he lived in Boston, I ask, "When did you first fall in love?"

"In college," Jack answers, without hesitation. He was so madly in love that he transferred colleges to be with her. But within days of Jack's new start, he received a letter. She'd changed her mind—about Jack, about the college, and then the worst: she admitted to being involved with one of Jack's best friends.

"Nothing hurts as much as losing your first love."

He gives a half-shrug. "It was a long time ago." Jack glances over his shoulder.

"What?"

"Did you see that white car backing up over there?" he asks.

"No. Why?"

"It was my ex-girlfriend."

"Nadia lives around here?"

"Nope."

"Do you think she saw us?"

"Pretty sure, yes."

I begin to feel uneasy. "So now what?"

"I'll probably get a text from her," he says. I guess, after fourteen years, he knows her well.

"Are you two friends?"

"She wants to be. But I don't know how that works. I say to her, 'What—we're going to get together with the new people we date?'" Jack checks his phone. "As predicted," he announces, smiling. "Incoming text from Nadia. 'I saw you walking with your new girlfriend. You make a beautiful couple. I wish you every happiness.'"

"Well, that was nice of her."

He begins texting and glances at me devilishly.

"What did you say?"

"Thank you for not running us over."

Later, when we're strolling through Boston Common, he stops three times to give homeless people money. While shopping on Newbury Street, he's helpless in the clutches of an aggressive saleswoman pressuring him to buy a five-thousand-dollar suede jacket. At lunch, he talks to the toddler at the table next to us. He tells me he visits his mother and stepfather in an assisted living facility every Sunday afternoon.

"You're a man of contradictions, Mr. Carver," I say.

"Not necessarily. I don't really know who I am." This admission shocks me the most, perhaps, not to mention the fact that Jack seems unperturbed by it.

♥

After dinner, we wander back to my hotel and have a drink in the lounge where a pianist plays jazz. We settle in with single malt scotch and listen.

"Why do you think you never married?" I ask.

"I never intended not to," Jack answers.

"What do you think it is?"

"I spent the early part of my career moving frequently. There were some special women I'd met. A while ago, I counted and I realize that there's been a special five."

"Interesting," I say. "A 'Special Five'?" I ask, making air quotes.

"There was one woman named Holly. I met her in Washington, DC. But when I told her I was going to be transferred out of DC back to Boston, she said she wasn't going to date me."

"She sounds smart," I say, laughing.

Jack talks about the Special Five, each woman in excruciating detail, for what feels like a long time. "All right. I don't need to hear about the Special Five ever again." And I surprise myself with the sharpness and intensity with which I say it, and the look on Jack's face tells me he's heard it, too.

♥

Date #22: On the Threshold

It's Sunday morning, and we're saying goodbye in the hotel lobby. He is off to see his mother, and I'll take a taxi to the train station. We kiss and thank each other for the weekend. He turns to walk out the door but then stops in the threshold, turning back to look at me. Our eyes meet one last time. It's because of that look I'm not worried. I know I will hear from him again.

That night, I'm home alone in my pajamas, reading, when he texts:

Jack: You arrived?

Me: I have, thanks. How's your mom?

Jack: Better this week.

Me: I'm glad. And I'm enjoying getting to know you.

Jack: With all my warts and idiosyncrasies!

Me: No one is one-dimensional. It keeps it interesting. We are remarkably honest with each other. That's something I enjoy about us.

Jack: Sleep well.

I think of Evan. I couldn't tolerate his idiosyncrasies, even after just a few dates. They were beyond annoying already. For some reason, Jack's don't bother me.

♥

Today, as we're driving home from school, I ask Evie, "In the past year, what have you learned about love?"

She pauses a few seconds. "You can't really choose who you love."

"I think you're right!"

"And love can trick you," she continues. "Love can shoot you in the stomach and make you sad."

"You mean like Cupid?" I say.

"Yeah."

Out of the mouths of babes. "You know, the Greeks and the Romans thought of it exactly like that. Cupid just shoots his arrow and you're done. Out of your control. What else?"

"Sometimes love makes you panic. Sometimes people don't love you back. It's very tedious."

"Tedious! How do you know that word? That's an awesome word!"

"Yeah . . . I know that word . . ."

"You are one smart girl, Evie. It sure is tedious."

Speaking of tedium, it's early June, and these days I still spend too much time thinking about Jack. He mentioned he was in New York City for a few days this week at a conference and yet has not made any suggestion we get together, even though I live less than an hour away. It stings a bit. I'd take just a hug, a kiss, a quick drink, a minute to connect. But he obviously doesn't feel that way. But then, by late in the week, once he's back in Boston, he asks what I'm doing next weekend.

I say I'm in New York, going to dinner and theater with Luke and then staying the weekend at a hotel.

"That sounds interesting," Jack says.

"You're welcome to stay with me."

"But I wouldn't want to be presumptuous," Jack says.

Jack tells me he'll be in Wisconsin at the end of the week and will fly in to New York to join me.

"I'd love to see you," I say. And that, of course, is an understatement.

♥

CHAPTER 12

Only Time to Live

Date #23: Banana Bread & Mormons

This date with Jack is supposed to have begun yesterday. I've booked us a room at my favorite New York City hotel, The Gramercy Park, but as I'm checking in, Jack calls from Wisconsin, his voice tight. "They've canceled my flight," he says. "Thunderstorms. All three airports—LaGuardia, JFK, Newark—are either closing or closed."

"Ugh." I'm not entirely surprised; the sky outside tells the story. Massive thunderstorms are plaguing the entire New York area. "But we've got tickets to *The Book of Mormon*," I say.

"I'm well aware of that. Not a lot I can do."

Texts and phone calls back and forth the rest of the evening. Finally, Jack says, "I've got a plan. I've rented a car, I'm driving to Chicago, and I'm booked on a flight to LaGuardia tomorrow morning."

He's really trying. His heroic acts of chivalry are impressive, maybe even to the standards of Greg and the *Rules* ladies.

♥

Saturday morning is clear skies and sunshine. I walk to the Union Square farmers' market and buy strawberries and banana bread.

My stomach has been doing somersaults. The extent of my longing for him surprises me. Ever since our weekend in Boston, my feelings for him have only intensified, it's a blessing and a curse.

A little after 10:00 a.m., my phone rings. He's in a taxi, almost at the hotel.

I enter the dark, crimson lobby, my eyes adjusting to the dim. Even at this time of year, it still smells of wood smoke from the stone fireplace. I can't find him. "Where are you?" I text.

Then a deep voice: "Holly."

I turn around. His arms are around me. "You made it."

"I did."

"A valiant effort."

Back up in the room, Jack opens the champagne that the hotel has gifted us. He explodes it with a bang and I startle at the noise and we laugh. Champagne, strawberries, and banana bread—a breakfast picnic in bed with the sunlight sifting through the blinds.

And then our clothes come off. "Ahhh . . . skin!" Jack exclaims as our bodies twist around each other in the cool sheets. We fit perfectly.

"It's really good to see you," I say, and then I kiss him again. "I didn't know if you'd make it."

"It was touch and go . . ." Then we hear a noise. A key in the lock.

I freeze. "Did you hear that?" I say.

"Hey there!" Jack calls out.

"Sorry," a male voice answers—a voice of someone who is clearly in our room, just out of sight, but very close by. We hear the door close.

"Was that someone you gave a key to—from last night?" Jack says.

"I hope you are joking," I say. *Did he really just say that?*

Jack is kissing me again. Did he really just say that—and a wave of hurt starts to rise. *Let it go, Holly. Not now.* And for a time, I do let it go.

♥

We are showered and dressed for dinner. I'm collecting my things for the night to put in my evening bag—some lipstick, a credit card, a little cash, my phone. On the table is the room key. I pick it up and point the key toward Jack. "Do you really think I'd let someone else in?"

Jack is staring at the floor looking solemn.

"Look at me." The words come out in my stern voice, the one I use when Evie is in trouble.

His eyes meet mine. "No," he says quietly.

"I was here alone last night, *pining* for you." I turn my back and open the door. He follows. We walk to the elevator in silence. And then, as we ride down, we talk about the restaurant I've picked for dinner, as though nothing has happened.

The Book of Mormon is outrageously bawdy. Jack laughs loud and hard. It's funny for me, too, yet as the night goes on, it becomes more disturbing. While the laughter uplifts most, for me there is a darker underside. I see how I began this life indoctrinated with a world view so bizarre and with so little basis in reality, it's a laughing-stock. The realization hits me with force. A life of the absurd.

After the play, Jack and I go out for a night cap. I tell him about my childhood performing baptisms for the dead in the Mormon temple wearing a white polyester onesie with a giant zipper, from neck to crotch. "Kind of like an Elvis jumpsuit," I say, and Jack laughs again. And some of the Mormon rules for dating: not until you're sixteen. And when dancing, always stay a distance of at least one Book of Mormon apart.

"Height or width?" Jack wonders aloud.

♥

Date #24: As It Began

It's Sunday morning, and we make love for the third time in less than twenty-four hours. This time is the best. "Holly, Holly, Holly," he says with a sigh, collapsing next to me on the bed. He turns his head and kisses me tenderly on the cheek. We laze in bed, warm and at peace. I begin to drift off to sleep curled around him, feeling his skin on mine, the rise and fall of his chest. "You're like a bump on a log," Jack teases.

"I don't want to move," I mumble. I think of how incredible this feels to be with this person I care for and to enjoy each other in this way. I was raised to be ashamed of this and was taught that these pleasures were wrong.

We linger in bed and he tells me stories, his thoughts on so many things. He talks a lot about his past, rarely the future.

Late morning, we get out of bed and head to Lupa in the Village for lunch. Walking alongside Jack, holding hands, it feels natural, as though there's no other place for me to be. I almost forget this weekend is nearly over.

The weather is warm, so we sit outside, eating pasta, drinking wine, relaxed. We talk about the pets we had as children. "My first pet was a deaf tabby cat. Then a duck," I say.

Jack says his friend's mother, dressed to the nines for a formal event, accidentally impaled the family cat on her stiletto heel as she descended the staircase, making her grand entrance in front of the family.

"Kitten heels!" I say. "Horrible!" And then I tell him about my former father-in-law accidentally shooting the family's golden retriever in front of his three children during target practice.

"I think we're even on the tragic pet stories," Jack says.

We head back to the hotel and pause in the red velvet lobby with the Venetian chandelier, where a fire has been lit, and say goodbye amid the smell of wood smoke, just as the weekend began.

Jack is gone in a cab to Penn Station where he will catch the train back to Boston.

I ask the hotel concierge to let me into Gramercy Park. The park is private and accessible to local residents and hotel guests only. The bellman walks me across the street and opens the tall, black iron gate with a key. "How will I get out?" I ask, eyeing the spiked fence that looks too high to climb.

He hands me his card. "You call me and I'll come get you," he answers, locking me in.

I'm in my little park prison. Two elderly women walk slowly down the gravel path together, hunched over canes, one with just one pant leg rolled up to the knee.

I lay across two benches under the shade of a very old tree, its trunk deep and ridged and brown, and watch two squirrels chase each other through the branches. The sunlight sifts through the leaves; the air is perfect.

I remember that I've tucked the last of the banana bread into Jack's briefcase. I wonder if he's found it. It's the first girlfriendy thing I've done.

A low, sad feeling has returned. For a second, I think that I can't keep doing this. The sinking vulnerability of wanting someone badly, not knowing if and when and how we'll see each other again.

Jack is the only man in my life now. He's the one I want, but you can't always get what you want, or at least not right away, and of course, we are not exclusive. I know I need to be patient and keep dating and try to meet other people, but it feels like a chore. Like doing laundry or flossing your teeth—good for you, prudent.

Later that night, I head to Sfoglia on the Upper East Side and eat dinner at the bar. A couple in their mid-sixties, Max and Mimi, strike up a conversation. Max is a native New Yorker, short, wrinkled, and smiling. Mimi has a wide, warm face with porcelain skin and very blue eyes; she's outgoing, from rural Pennsylvania originally. After her kids left home and went to college, she surprised everyone by divorcing her husband and moving to New York City and starting her life over with Max.

We talk about raising kids. I tell them that the other day Evie asked "What's a boner, Mom?" and they laugh hysterically. Evie heard the word on the school bus and wondered if women got them, too. "Is it like wood?" she asked.

Mimi and I talk about feminism and what it means these days. Both she and Max encourage me to write about this stage in life. We talk about how the person you want to grow old with may be different from the person you have children with. They look at each other, lock eyes, and agree.

Max has grown quiet and has been listening to Mimi and me talk for a while. I've been telling Mimi about Jack. Max looks me in the eye and says, "The fact that you told us about his age says something. Trust your instinct. You know this is a problem."

You know this is a problem.

Max's candor startles me. "I will think about that. Thank you," I say.

Then Max adds that Mimi's sister married a much older man. She's now simultaneously dealing with an ill, aging husband and raising a teenager. "It's a hard life for her," Max says.

♥

It's afternoon, and as I go outside to check the mail, I discover a giant moth on the front porch. She's celadon green, large, yet delicate, shaped like some sort of ghostly stealth bomber. Never in my life have I seen anything quite like this ethereal creature and I wonder what it might be. After some research, I learn she's a Luna moth.

I bring Evie outside and show her the moth and she, too, is in awe. I tell her what I've learned—that Luna moths are elusive and not often seen during the day and are attracted to the moon as a source of light. They supposedly signify rebirth and new beginnings. Because they gravitate toward the light in the darkness of night, the Luna moth is seen as a symbol of spiritual transformation, heightened awareness; a striving toward truth. I tell Evie that the moth will only live a week. "One week? That's so sad."

"She doesn't even have a mouth. She only has time to live."

David has texted that his girlfriend, Adrienne, who he's been dating for over two years now, will be picking up Evie today on his behalf. This is the first time that Adrienne has come to my home, by herself, without David. The last time I saw her in close proximity was across the table in a law office, in deposition, as a court reporter hammered out Adrienne's halting sentences, word for word, for the record. David asks if I'm okay with the arrangements, and I tell him I'm comfortable. I like Adrienne. She's a mother of two teenage girls, and from what I can tell, she treats Evie like one of her own. She's an innocent, like Evie, caught in the crossfire between David and me. The day that Evie told me that she saw Adrienne sneaking around David's yard on Easter Sunday at 6:30 in the morning in her pink bathrobe, setting up an Easter egg hunt for Evie, I thought, *This Adrienne is okay.* Even more endearing given the fact that Adrienne is Jewish and doesn't even celebrate Easter.

Adrienne and her youngest daughter ring the doorbell. Evie bounds to the door, flings it open, and hugs them both. Evie pulls them over to see the moth that's still resting on the spindled porch railing. The four of us cluster around, marveling at her beauty. And I marvel, too, at these new people who have come into our lives and how we are all finding our way toward a new beginning.

Before dark, I check outside, and the moth has flown away.

♥

Date #25: Snow White and the Seven Gourds

Chip has big cheeks, and the skin at his jaw line hangs over his collar. But he has a warm smile and he's tall and apparently smart—he went to MIT.

Chip uses the word *transparent* a lot, probably because he's a management consultant. If I ask him a personal question, like why his engagement failed to the woman he said had "looks, body, and career," he says cheerfully, "Okay, I can be transparent!"

"What's the most bizarre date you've been on?" I ask him next.

"Ahh!" Chip says, smiling at the memory. His face has turned an alarming shade of deep tomato since he began his second beer, and I start to wonder if I should ask about his blood pressure. "Her profile said that she worked in the legal profession. I thought she was a lawyer," he says.

"Okay," I say, egging him on.

"But she was an office manager, and she spent the first part of the date talking about how she was in Kinkos all day at the photocopier."

"Makin' copies!" I say, like the Richmeister from *Saturday Night Live*. Chip stares at me like I have a head injury and proceeds with his story.

"My father said that you have to dance with the girl that you take to the dance, so I tried to get to know her. I asked her what she did in her spare time." Chip pauses for effect.

My eyes widen. "Which was . . .?"

"She goes into her briefcase and pulls out a large sketch pad. 'I like to paint pumpkins,' she says."

"What?"

"Yup, she paints pumpkins. She paints them with all sorts of figures, like Snow White and Bugs Bunny, etcetera."

"Wow," I say. "Did you go out again?"

"I called her the next day and told her there wouldn't be a second date and I tried to lighten it up by saying it was because she didn't have any Elmer Fudd sketches."

I laugh. "Did she find that funny?"

"Nope, she didn't find it funny," Chip says, cracking himself up.

Speaking of Elmer Fudd. In the end, there's no Elmer line delivered, instead I take the chickenshit/tried-and-true Luke method. The gentle text. What's becoming my standard: first, I say my thank-yous. Thank you for taking the time to meet and thank you for treating me to a drink, a meal, a sandwich, a coffee, a cheese stick, etcetera. And then the part about the lack of spark and best wishes for finding your special someone. Argh. Am I starting to sound jaded?

♥

Date #26: All the Dough

It's barely summer, and this day is already hot. This calls for a sundress and sandals.

The plan is to meet Desmond at a Starbucks at 11:00 a.m. Another online date.

We sit outside in a courtyard under the shade of trees. Within a minute or two, I can see something is off, but it's hard to put my finger on it. He's not hard on the eyes, but he's odd, somehow. His hair swirls in thick, dark waves, with just the slightest touch of gray. He looks at me directly at first, but then stares off into the distance as he talks, almost as though I'm not there. His brown eyes dart back and forth like he's watching a tennis match that no one else can see.

He tells me that he works as a consultant to financial institutions out of his apartment in a nearby town. The town he's in has some rough areas and I wonder why he's chosen to live there. "Do you rent or own your apartment?" I ask.

"Rent. My wife took all the money."

"Ahh . . ." I say, smiling weakly.

"I'm good with clients, just not bosses," he says.

He talks rapidly. He tells me that his brother is a famous plastic surgeon in Beverly Hills. Then he changes the subject to talking about his daughter getting into college.

I watch his mouth moving. He has white stuff at the sides and bottom of his mouth, like stringy dough. I listen some more and then I say, "When you're not with your kids, what do you like to do?"

"I read. So, my daughter is also looking to apply to some select schools in the South . . ."

So much for social cues. Eventually he finishes talking about his daughter. Now it's onto his ex-wife. "I try not to hate her," he says, smiling, with what seems a touch of menace. She's a real estate agent, he tells me, squinting at her office, which happens to be exactly across the street. I wonder if she can see us right now. Is she here? I glance around, but no one is staring at us.

He confesses that he knew he shouldn't have married her, that they had lived together for five years and he felt the pressure. "Our friends' wedding invitations would come in the mail and I would dread giving them to her. 'Why aren't we getting married?' she'd always ask," he says.

Ted Bundy! That's who this guy reminds me of! Ted Bundy!

I look at my watch. I throw back the last of my cappuccino and stand. "I need to go. Nice meeting you," I say, patting him on the shoulder. He has a look of shock on his face. I start walking and I don't look back.

♥

It's a Friday night in late June and I'm out here in the woods, home alone. I've been "good" and haven't texted Jack since Monday night. That fact that I'm still focused on what's a natural communication between us just pisses me off. Is it me, him, or both?

He called me on Wednesday night. Then tonight, in a moment of weakness, I call him at 9:00. He doesn't answer. I hang up without leaving a message. Calling a man on a Friday night is the biggest dating violation ever. I am pathetic. It's not just the communication that's the issue; I'm still at the where-do-I-stand issue. And when will we see each other again? After nearly four months of dating, I still don't have a read on us.

The Rules chicks would say time to go hardcore: no texting, ignore his ass unless he suggests getting together again. No initiating anything. But do I have that kind of strength?

I've stayed home tonight because I've got some legal and financial loose ends to complete from my divorce. I go into my study and settle in at my desk, working through a spreadsheet. The numbers swim before my eyes and I try to focus but it's not easy. I decide, instead, that I'll just deal with the piles of papers on the floor. These should be put away. Papers I should lock up in case Evie finds them. Papers about custody, papers about my legal battles with her father. What if Evie is like me? Curious, a sleuth, seeking my own answers. Just a few years older than Evie, I found my parents' love letters, the cards and the court transcripts hidden in a box under the stairs in the basement.

The love letters and the cards that show the longing when they're apart, the passion, pet names and private jokes, and their years of history.

The deposition depicts a bitter battle. What happened to them? Why did Dad leave? Was this all about his other woman? The judge reads my name aloud in court: minor child, Holly Annabelle. Next, my sister: Margot Helena. "Are these your daughters?" the judge asked.

"That's what she tells me," the transcript states my father answered. We're not his? Mom says that, as a toddler, I would stand at the window every evening waiting for him to come home. Why did you leave us, Dad?

There's a tapping at my window. It scares me a little at first, but I pull back the curtain and see that it's a large moth, it's the Luna moth, fluttering up against the glass, drawn to the light. She's still alive! I watch her for a while and then let the curtain fall back. As I work at my desk, she's still there, fluttering up a storm, wings beating an urgent rhythm. She is drawn to the light; she is not giving up. It's as though she's telling me to keep going, keep going.

♥

Jack never returned my call from Friday night. I realize that I shouldn't expect him to read my mind, and I need to be an adult and speak up. I need to tell him that I'm not feeling good about things between us anymore.

I need to say that after he left New York without saying anything about getting in touch or when we might see each other again, it felt cold and it hurt. And rather than putting that in a text or ignoring him altogether, I figure I'll be mature about it and communicate that directly.

I play John Mayer's "Say" to psych myself up. I laugh at myself, and cringe too, that I'm so scared to have a conversation, so afraid to talk to a boy (a sixty-something "boy") and use my words. "*Say what you need to say . . .*"

I dial, my pulse quickening. He doesn't answer so I leave a message. Ugh. I hope I sound even. A short time later he calls back, twice.

The first time, he is on his way to the barber to get his haircut. It's awkward, we make small talk and then he says he has to call me later.

He calls a second time, three hours later, and we finally have the talk. I struggle to get the words out, but I do. I say that we had this amazing weekend together and then he left—and I really have no idea where we stand these days, when we'll get together again.

"Really?" he says. There is a dog barking in the background. "See, the dog hates me, too."

"I don't hate you." But I add that things between us aren't making me happy anymore. "I thought to myself—what does this man think of me? It stung when you made the joke about me letting someone else in the hotel room."

"I'm sorry," Jack says.

"I feel like you don't value me."

"I don't even value myself," he says. Long pause. "Sorry, I shouldn't have said that."

"It's okay." *Wow.* "Well, I feel better just having said it. Getting it off my chest."

"You have a beautiful chest."

"You and I can talk about pretty much anything. Except us. You know, I don't know why I have such a hard time with talking. You'd think at my age I'd be better at it."

"I'm not any better at my age," Jack says.

"I miss you."

"You are a lovely woman." And it's the end of conversation. Nothing is resolved, he's given me scant reassurance, but at least I've expressed my feelings. Somehow that helps.

♥

CHAPTER 13

Shiny Red Trucks

It's early July, and I'm back in California sitting outside at a restaurant. A couple nearby holds a baby. An older woman walks by and calls out, "Beautiful baby! Did you ever know you could love anything so much?" So true. I've never loved anyone more than Evie.

Later that night, I have a drink at a wine bar and a young guy named Bobby strikes up a conversation. He's there with his friend Stella.

I ask Bobby if Stella is his girlfriend, and Bobby shakes his head. Stella isn't listening, she's chatting with some other guy sitting next to her. She's got the hot librarian look—long, dark wavy hair with dark-framed glasses.

Bobby confides that Stella is engaged to a famous and very wealthy movie producer. She's twenty-five, he's sixty-three.

"What do you think of the relationship?" I ask.

"I'm annoyed—because at first she lied about it," he says in a low tone. "Said the guy was her 'mentor.'"

Is Bobby a little jealous?

Bobby goes on to say that the producer bought Stella a small public relations firm in town to give her something to do.

"Just a little business to keep her busy?"

"Yep," Bobby answers, again seeming miffed. Then he tells me that the movie producer's friends were giving him crap that Stella is simply after his money. So, the producer writes Stella a check for $1 million free and clear to "even" the playing field. Here's the money, go if you want, he says. "She's still around," Bobby says.

"It's an interesting idea. I've never heard of such a thing," I say.

Bobby is in his late twenties and originally from St. Louis. He went to boarding school in the east and is now an executive of a tech start-up. I mention Sheryl Sandberg's book *Lean In* and he knows it. He says the tough thing about managing women is that if they have a disagreement, they will carry a grudge forever. "Are men any different?" I ask.

"I think so. Or at least they let it go. It's just business."

"So, what do you do in that situation?" I ask.

"I try to create incentives for two women pissed off at each other to help each other again in the future."

"Smart."

Bobby asks me if I would come to his company and on the lunch hour speak to his staff about my former business life. He says they have business people in all the time from other industries so they can learn from them. "That's really flattering," I say. "Let me think about it," and we exchange phone numbers.

Yes, weird and flattering to be asked by a twenty-something to share my knowledge. He must see me as an "elder."

Date #27: Hanging Out?

I get a text from twenty-something high-tech Bobby. "Drink tonight?" he asks.

"Okay," I answer.

Is this a date? Do twenty-somethings even date? I don't think they even use that word; they just "hang out." Maybe this is an invitation to hang out. He's smart, cute, and fun. I'm not doing anything otherwise.

Bobby and I meet up at a bar and have a couple of drinks. He gets the first round, I buy the second. So again, I'm thinking, is this a date? Even in the dim light, Bobby doesn't look a day over twenty-five. Completely boyish with brown bangs hanging into his eyes, even a smattering of freckles. While cute and bright, he keeps checking his phone every five minutes. Annoying, but I suppose this is what guys his age do.

After a while, I tell Bobby I need to get going. He looks up from his phone. "Can I share a cab with you?" he asks. He tells me that his apartment is on the way to my house. I agree.

In the cab, Bobby puts his hand on my knee. "What are you doing?" I say with some amusement. Then he takes my hand and squeezes it. *He can't possibly be interested in me. I'm old enough to be his mother!* And then he leans in to give me an open-mouthed kiss. I pull back. "Do you want to come in?" he says. We've arrived at his apartment.

You have got to be kidding me. I want to start laughing, and yet I'm also flattered. "Sorry, no," I manage to mumble. I am not even remotely tempted.

"Can I come over later?" he asks.

I shake my head. "Sorry."

He waves good night as the cab pulls away.

As I ride back to my house, I smile. Wow. The kid has balls. And interesting taste in women. And I suppose the lesson here is if you wonder if it could be a date, then it probably is.

♥

Date # 28: License and ID, Please

Dating—putting yourself out there—can feel like hard work. At times, it gets downright tiring and demoralizing. I decide the best place to grab dinner tonight is probably The Starling again. There's a community feel and the moody, broody part of me wants to revisit the places that Jack and I have been. It was here that we first met. I'm still uneasy about us. Our recent conversation about where we stand seems to have had some impact—he called and asked me if I'd join him in Nantucket in three weeks and I've agreed to go. But three weeks seems far in the future especially since I've hardly heard from him since.

When I arrive at the restaurant, I nab the very seat I sat in that first night. To my right, instead of Jack, is a woman who is dining with her husband, nestled in close, talking quietly. I'm envious, and it just underscores how much I miss him. I finish my dinner alone and decide to retrace my steps even further and return to Black's, the R&B bar.

Like that first night, blasting blues can be heard from a block away. I squeeze through a thick crowd and order a drink. Huddling in a far corner I stare toward the room where we'd sat. *What is Jack doing tonight?*

"Are you mad?" someone says. A man I've never seen before stands in front of me. He's African American and strikingly good-looking.

"What?"

"Are you mad?" he repeats.

"No. Why?"

"Well, you look mad!" he says.

Do I have resting bitch face? "I'm not mad," I tell the man, and then I realize I'm not mad, I'm actually just plain sad.

"Today is my birthday," he says, smiling. He's very tall and lean. Maybe a professional athlete?

"Is it really your birthday?" I ask. He pulls out his wallet and hands me his driver's license and sure enough, it is. He was born in 1981, which makes him thirty-three.

Thirty-three! "Happy birthday . . ." I study the card again in the dim light. "Graham."

"Thanks. I'm out celebrating with some guys from the station and some other friends."

"Station?"

"Yeah, I'm a firefighter."

"Really?"

Graham shakes his head, sighing dramatically, and reaches for his wallet again, producing a firefighter identification card. He's local. "Well, you got me again," I say. "How long have you been a firefighter?"

"Seven years. Come over and hang out with us," Graham says, gesturing to a group of about ten men and women.

"Is everyone in your group a firefighter?"

"No, we've got some paramedics and nurses and a couple of wives and girlfriends."

"Do you have a wife or a girlfriend?"

Graham grins. "No. And I don't have ID for that. C'mon," he says. Before I know it, everyone is introducing themselves and welcoming me. They're an incredibly warm group of people, and I think about how these are all front-line folks, first responders who put their lives on the line and care for people every day. It stands to reason they're friendly. We finish our drinks and someone says, "Next bar!" and we head a few doors down to a brew pub. After beers, it's announced that we're next walking to a nightclub, ten minutes away.

The night is warm, and everyone laughs and jokes as we make our way. I'm feeling no pain now, and my spirits have improved considerably. I'm really having fun. "So a fireman, huh?" I say to Graham, who seems to be making a point of walking next to me.

"Yup." He's got an easy confidence, maybe even a little swagger, yet somehow, he's shy, too.

"Can you do the fireman's carry?" The words are hardly out of my mouth before Graham has flipped me upside down over his shoulder and is now carrying me to the club, upside down, caveman-style. I'm yelling for him to put me down and everyone is laughing. "Okay! You're definitely a fireman!" Graham stops and gently returns me to my feet.

"When are you going to learn to just believe me?" Graham says.

At the club, Graham squeezes in next to me in a booth and the champagne begins to flow. Everyone toasts Graham's thirty-third. He and I talk of how often I'm in California, his job, his friends.

"Do you want to dance?" Graham asks me.

"I really should get going. I have a daughter and she's with a babysitter."

"Let me help you get a taxi," Graham says.

Outside, there's a line of taxis and Graham hugs me. "Happy birthday—you really cheered me up," I say and then I jump in a cab.

By the time I'm home, there's a text from Graham asking if I arrived safely. I tell him all's well. "I really like you. When do I see you next?" he asks. I don't reply. This gorgeous young man will have forgotten me by morning.

♥

Wrong. Next morning, there's a new text from Graham:

> **Graham**: Seriously, when can I see you again?
> **Me**: Oh Graham, you're incredibly handsome, but I should tell you I'm way too old for you! I'm 45.
> **Graham**: I don't care. You're beautiful and I like your company.
> **Me**: Aren't you nice.
> **Graham**: Sometimes.
> **Me**: Ha!
> **Graham**: I like that you're older. Maybe you can teach me something new.
> **Me**: I'm going to need to think about this. I'm torn.
> **Graham**: Why torn?
> **Me**: Our age difference and I'm seeing someone. He and I aren't exclusive but maybe soon. I'm back in CA in August. Can I get back in touch if I'm officially 100% single?
> **Graham**: Age schmage. Blah.

What am I doing with this "seeing someone" line of defense? And this Graham. As stunning as he is, there's a difference between dating someone six years your junior versus twice that. I realize that men do it all the time and no one bats an eye when a man dates a woman ten or even twenty years younger, but I am torn. I didn't see this coming.

♥

Date #29: The Man Cave

Graham is charming and persistent, and he's successfully eroding my resolve to wait till August to see him again. He texts that he really wants to get together, but he's been mandated to work today. He's got no choice in the matter. That happens with firefighters and other emergency personnel, he explains. "No worries," I say. I ask if he can step away for a quick lunch or coffee and he says that's not how it works. There aren't scheduled breaks, and you must be physically present at all times for not only fires, but emergency medical calls, which he handles and are more frequent. "Come by the station—I'll give you a tour," Graham says.

I haven't toured a fire station since I was in kindergarten.

When I arrive, I find Graham on the street level in the garage, with all the fire trucks. He's in uniform, wearing a short-sleeved navy-blue button-down shirt and matching pants. Some of the other firefighters I recognize from the other night are there. The Captain smiles and Graham introduces me again. I'm feeling a little self-conscious now.

"It's Monday, so that means we do maintenance on the equipment," Graham says, all business-like. "Let me show you one of the trucks." As he opens the large red door, revealing an impressive array of equipment, I notice his arms—muscled biceps and a pronounced vein snaking through flawless, coffee-colored skin. "These trucks run a million a piece."

Graham leads me toward the back of the station. "So we always need to check that these tanks are filled," he says, picking up an oxygen tank.

"What's that thing here?" I ask, pointing to what look like large, sharp, shears. "Is it 'the jaws of life' or something?"

"Exactly. It's used to for cutting metal—usually car accidents."

I watch Graham inspect the equipment. I can see he loves what he does and takes it very seriously. He's a Boy Scout with the preparedness and all.

Next he leads me upstairs into to the second level of the firehouse and we stand in the kitchen. There are three large stainless-steel refrigerators. "Do you guys cook for yourselves?" I ask.

"Oh yeah, my captain is really into cooking. We have great food here. A lot of the time, he assigns us stuff to make."

"Like what?"

"Calzones. Homemade."

"Pastry and everything?"

"Yep," Graham says.

"Captain Calzone!"

"Then through here . . ." Graham says, leading me to the next room, "is the TV room."

I crack up. Arranged in a semi circle around a TV the size of a billboard are a dozen recliners. "This is a serious man cave! You each have your own recliner?"

"Yup," Graham says.

"I won't ask how you guys decide who controls the remote."

"Usually the captain," Graham says. Then I follow Graham around a corner. "And here is my room."

"For some reason, I imagined you were all together in bunk beds, right around the fire pole?"

He laughs. "Nope. We get the same room every shift."

I stand at the doorway and look in. It's simple with a bed, some lockers, and a chest of drawers. Graham locks eyes with me, an amused smile on his face. I stare back at him, smiling now, too. My God. Then we hear the sound of a door closing and male voices. "Come on," Graham says. "Let's go out this way."

Graham takes me down a side staircase and walks me outside to my car. "I'll text you," he says. "Let's figure out when we can get together." We give each other a hug, and as I drive away, he grins and waves. *Damn.*

♥

Date #30: R & R

Summertime in California, a beautiful night, and I'm out for the first time with my new friend, Fern. We're talking to two single dads who have bought us drinks at a wine bar.

The tallest and most attractive of the pair has looks reminiscent of a modern Elvis, with slicked back dark hair. He's Rhett and he's taken a shine to Fern. That leaves me with his buddy, Ryan, who is completely bald, wiry, and raisin-toned from beach volleyball, which he plays several times a week. While I'm not exactly attracted to Ryan, he's funny as hell and has been making me laugh for an hour. He gives me his card, suggests we get together, but I've politely dodged, avoiding a definitive answer. "Guys, I need to call it a night," I say.

"Already?" Fern says. Her cheeks are flushed, and Rhett's arm is draped over her spaghetti-strapped shoulders.

"Yeah. I'm tired. How are you getting home?" I ask her.

"We can drive her home," Rhett says. "You too."

"But I'm the other direction. I'll get a cab." I study Fern. She seems clear-headed enough and these two guys seem trustworthy. "You sure you don't want to share a cab with me?" I ask Fern again.

"It's okay," she answers with a little wink and so I say good night and head home.

♥

My phone is ringing the next morning as I'm having my first cup of coffee. "Thank God I backed up my phone!" Fern says when I pick up.

"Why?"

"I lost my phone! I think I left it in Ryan's car when they drove me home. You've got his number, right?"

"Hang on." I shuffle out of bed and find my handbag. "Yup," I say, staring at the white card with the black and red print.

"Do you mind calling him and getting him to check his car?"

"Sure."

"Well, *hellll-oooo!*" Ryan says when he answers. I start laughing. Just his tone of voice is farcical.

"Fern just called . . ."

"She did, did she—"

"Yeah. She thinks she left her phone in your car."

"What a ruse! You're just too bashful to say you're calling because you want to go out with me, aren't you?"

I snort. "No. That's not why I'm calling."

"Oh. Oh. That hurts . . ."

"Fern really thinks she left her phone in your car last night. Would you mind checking?"

"Not at all," Ryan says.

"That would be great—"

"But only if you promise to go out with me again."

"Um . . ."

"What? I sense some hesitation? Some shyness . . .?"

I laugh nervously. "There's no free lunch, is there?"

"Actually, I was thinking dinner. Or a drink tonight?"

"I might be able to do a drink."

"What else did Fern tell you about her ride home last night?"

"Nothing, other than losing the phone."

Ryan hoots. "Your friend Fern was MAKING OUT on the hood of my car!" "You're making that up!"

"Oh, yes she did! She was my little hood ornament!"

"No . . ."

"I sat there in my car, the engine running, watching the whole thing as she and Rhett made out on the hood of my car. Like I wasn't even there. I feel a little dirty."

"My God, that's funny."

"You know there's some things you just can't unsee," Ryan says.

"Wow. So they're an item, then?"

"Oh, I don't know if I'd say that," he says, laughing harder.

"Fern must have been drunker than I thought. 'Course I don't know her that well."

"See the fun you missed?" Ryan asks.

"Apparently."

"I'm going to check my car for the phone and I'll text you. And we'll figure out where we're doing tonight," Ryan says gleefully.

"Sounds like I don't have a choice."

♥

Date #31: Mythic Beasts & Sin City

Ryan: Not in the back. Not in the front.

Me: Check the hood?

Ryan: My darling, you are the new bowsprit for the hood of my car!

Me: Ha!

Ryan and I meet at a tapas bar. He's wearing a baseball cap and shorts. The one glass of Spanish red turns into two, two turn into a few. We start talking and do not stop. He makes me laugh so hard I have a mild asthma attack and need to excuse myself to go to the ladies' room to use my inhaler.

"So are you seeing anyone?" Ryan asks when I return.

"Yes. It's a bit complicated."

"How can it be complicated with you, darling? He must worship the ground you walk on."

I sigh heavily and reach for my wine. *Jack.* "No, not even close. We've been dating a few months, we're not exclusive, but . . ."

"But what, beautiful?"

"We're going to Nantucket together in a couple of weeks."

"I see," Ryan says.

"He lives in Boston. How about you?"

"Oh, I have some women that I see," Ryan says, smirking. "No one I'm serious about."

In the parking lot, heading home, our mood is light again. As Ryan opens the car door for me, I say, "Do you ever take that thing off?" He's still wearing his baseball cap. I whip it off his head and toss it in the air.

"Hey!" he yells just as it lands in a nearby tree. We laugh hysterically and fumble around in the dark, trying to find a way to knock it off an upper branch, but it's stuck. We decide then to return to The Starling, and end up marching into the kitchen to ask if we can borrow a broom. The dishwashers look at us like we're nuts, which only makes us laugh harder. Ryan boosts me up, I bat the broom above my head, and eventually we get the thing down. Ryan scoops it off the ground and slaps it on my head.

"I look ridiculous in baseball caps!" I screech, whipping it off.

"No, baby, you in my hat is *hot!*"

"I look like a Sasquatch!" And we are laughing like idiots again.

Ryan drives me home and halfway there he hits the bakes and stops the car. "What?" I say.

"Let's go to Vegas," he says.

"Vegas? I've never been."

"Let's get married!"

"You are completely crazy!"

"I'd marry you. I would. Let's go to Vegas right now." He pauses. *Is he serious?*

"No more marriage!" I yell like a war cry. Ryan hits the gas again.

At the gate to my house, we say good night and he kisses me. It's not terrible. Not terrible at all. We talk of seeing each other again when I'm next in California. I admit I'll be in Boston later in the week visiting Jack, but we'll stay in touch.

That night as I crawl into bed feeling giddy and still a little wheezy from laughing so much, I'm glad I took a chance and went out with Ryan. There's more to him than I originally thought.

♥

The next morning, I see that Ryan hasn't slept much. A text from 4:37 a.m.:

Ryan: We have ourselves a serious problem . . .

Then at 6:29 a.m.:

Xoxox
Wow!!!

Midmorning, I text back:

What an evening! Thank you.
Ryan: "What an evening!" is that a good thing? Or is that response more akin to what one might feel after surviving a plane crash?
Me: It was a great night! Truly.
Ryan: I'm a little worried . . . truly . . .
Me: We played keep-away with your hat. And you called me a Yeti but don't we need to get to know each other better? We just met.
Ryan: I know all I need to know . . .
I can't remember why I said Yeti, but there was a funny reason . . .
Me: I said I look like a Sasquatch in baseball caps.
Ryan: Ah . . .Then I'm wildly attracted to a folkloric, half man, half beast!
Me: An abiding image, as my poetry teacher used to say.
Ryan: You are my new favorite poem.
Me: That's very sweet.
Ryan: I'm going to pursue you. Love. This is what it's about.

Whoa.

♥

On the flight home with Evie, I see a familiar-looking face across the isle. The flight attendants are buzzing. I realize it's Robert F. Kennedy Jr.

"Evie," I whisper, "do you see that man over there?"

"Yeah. He shouldn't have his feet up on the back of the seat," she says. I crack up. Sure enough, RFK Jr. is in a suit and has taken off his shoes and socks, propping up his bare feet on the seat in front of him.

"Do you know who the Kennedys are?" I ask quietly.

"I think so. Like the airport?"

"Right. We're flying into JFK tonight, which stands for John F. Kennedy Airport, who was that man's uncle. You'll learn more about them someday."

As we fly east, I watch RFK Jr. work on the plane. Fingers curved around a pen, a stack of papers, it looks like a speech. Crossing out, writing in margins, setting the record straight. On his hand a wedding band, with some gold, some black.

His second wife and the mother of his children, distraught about their impending divorce, hung herself in the barn, fingers at the throat, as if she had changed her mind, but it was too late.

How does he do anything after that? And still he goes on, resilient, and marries a third time. Is it faith, belief in true love, or something else?

I watch him, thinking about all of his family's tragedies and his own and yet he has the courage to keep building, to commit again.

Where is my courage?

He orders "hot tea." Not a fan of the pretzel bread. Evie falls asleep on my shoulder and soon I drift off, too.

♥

CHAPTER 14

Under the Weather

Date #32: Cold

On the other side of the window, the summer rain spills in sheets. I'm on an afternoon train to Boston to see Jack.

Yesterday, I flew all day from the West Coast with Evie. She's with David for just one night so I'm back tomorrow. The fact that I'm willing to come this far for just a few hours says everything about my feelings for Jack. I'm jetlagged, Evie and I have both come down with terrible colds, my nose is red and running, my head full. Soon we'll be together in Nantucket, and yet I'm still on this train.

Jack said his townhouse renovation has begun, his place dusty and chaotic, that I'll be happier in a hotel. But unlike the first time I visited, he doesn't offer to make the arrangements. I'm on my own.

Jack finds me in the hotel lobby bar, ordering a hot whiskey toddy, which I hope will take the edge off the headache that's pounding between my eyes. He's coming from the office, dressed in his signature navy jacket and pale blue shirt. I put my arms around him but turn my head. "I've got a cold . . ."

"It's okay," he says, pressing his lips to mine.

"I don't want to—"

"Let's go upstairs."

In the room, there's an odd energy between us. I look and feel terrible, yet I'm so happy to see him, but at the same time, defensive. Jack keeps trying to pull me toward the bed, but I curl in the corner of the sofa, my black cotton dress pulled over my knees, a sweater wrapped around my shoulders, clutching my hot drink. I feel raw, and not just from being sick.

Jack slides his hand beneath my dress and leans in closer. I grab his wrist and shake my head. "I'm starving. I don't feel well. Let's get something to eat."

We walk to a nearby steakhouse for an early dinner. Two businessmen stop and say hello to Jack while we're eating. He doesn't bother to introduce me and we return to our steaks.

We go to bed early, and in the morning, I sit naked on the edge of the bed, the sheet wrapped around my shoulders. Showered, dressed, and ready for work, Jack sits down next to me. He kisses the top of my bare shoulder, my cheek, a kiss on the lips, and he is gone.

I stop at the hotel's front desk on the way to the station and find the bill unpaid. Of course. Why am I surprised, and why does it bother me? I can afford this.

By the afternoon, I'm back in Connecticut, still red-nosed and sick, more miserable than ever. Was Boston worth it? I don't know. I go to bed and fall into a deep sleep.

I'm awakened by the phone ringing. It's Jack, and by the time I've hung up, I'm further questioning my judgment on almost everything with that man. He wants me to meet his mother on Saturday.

♥

CHAPTER 15

Another Island

Date #33: A Man of Nantucket

Nantucket in July. White beaches with dunes and sea grass and brisk ocean breezes. Weathered-to-gray saltbox cottages and skies the color of the hydrangeas blooming everywhere.

We are staying in Nantucket's cobblestoned main town at the White Elephant. The resort overlooks the harbor and Children's Beach, and I am sitting outside on the lawn that is framed by flowerbeds of black-eyed Susans, enjoying a cold glass of wine and a book when Jack arrives. He sneaks up from behind and surprises me. I wrap my arms around his neck and kiss the little place behind his ear, his cheek, his mouth. He orders himself a beer, and I tell him about my trip from the airport with the Rasta taxi driver in a van straight out of *Scooby Doo*.

Jack has been coming here since he was a child, and his mother still owns a house on the island, but we are staying in a suite with an ocean view for privacy. There's a familiarity to our weekend hotel routine now. A little unpacking and chatter and flirtation, then a physical reconnection. The room is our respite, a Do Not Disturb sign dangling from the doorknob, warding off the outside world, heavy drapes drawn against the late afternoon sun, our bodies intertwined. We fall asleep in each other's arms.

Later, we dress for dinner and walk to a restaurant on the water owned by Jack's friends. We have cocktails steps away from a dock and moored boats that creak against ropes and the roll of the tide. We are seated at a table outdoors, with an ocean view and the fading light that has dimmed to shades of silver and blue. "I think they gave us the best table," he says, staring out at the water, and I agree.

Then the college-aged son of Jack's friends appears and announces that he will be our waiter. Jack leans back in his chair and a smile spreads across his face.

"Last time I saw you, you were about this tall," Jack says, holding his hand a few feet above the floor. "You're in college now?"

The waiter says he's studying economics at Dartmouth, and Jack approves. I think of Evie, too, and how before I know it, she'll be on her way in the world.

Jack is still smiling, looking after the waiter. He says, "That's a good kid. This is a family business."

"Did you ever want to have kids?"

"I never intended not to." Intended, *intention* . . . his answer gets me thinking. *What do I intend?* Fatherhood is something that's eluded him, even as much as he seems to say and do exactly what he wants. I wonder if he's always as in control as he presents himself.

Later, as we stroll back toward the hotel in the cool of the evening, a sweater and Jack's arm wrapped around my shoulders, he suggests a nightcap at The Club Car. The place is a Nantucket institution, a piano bar housed in a retrofitted railway car.

Jack and I squeeze in, literally. The long, narrow bar is absolutely jampacked with drinkers and revelers. He gets us drinks—God only knows what they are (and there's more than one round)—and I insist that we head in the direction of the piano to join in the sing-along. As we belt out Billy Joel's "Piano Man" together, I yell above the noise to Jack to say that he's got a good voice. He seems pleased and says that his mother says the same thing—she'd wanted him to pursue acting or singing.

His mother. I am meeting her tomorrow. I'm nervous—damn nervous—but the drink and the song distract me for now.

It's here that Jack introduces me to the evil that is the Espresso Martini. Vodka, Kahlua, espresso, and sugar. It's a killer, and goes down a little too easily.

At the end of the night, he guides me through the crowd and we bump up against a young woman, all lean limbs, short skirt, and spray tan. She's pretty drunk. She has one look at Jack and exclaims, "You're Jack Carver!"

He stops in his tracks and lifts an eyebrow. "Yes, I am," he says matter-of-factly and continues to move us through the crowd.

"Do you know her?" I ask.

"I don't think so."

"You're Jack Carver!" That scene will replay in my mind again and again in the coming weeks and months.

♥

Date #34: The Story of the Man Who Sleeps with My Mother

As I get ready for lunch, I study my bloodshot eyes in the bathroom mirror and wonder if I can get away with wearing sunglasses the entire time. Probably not. For most of the morning, Jack and I haven't spoken much. Intuitively, we understand that energy conservation is the priority. Today, I meet his mother.

We load into a taxi and head to the other side of the island, to the Wauwinet, a twenty-minute ride out of town.

Our driver is a frustrated Formula One driver. He takes each twist and turn at breakneck speed, and my stomach rises and lurches with each curve. *Do not throw up. Do not throw up. DoNotThrowUp.*

Lunch is outside on the patio near the water. Julia is already seated, her walker set aside. She's wearing a silk, turquoise blue dress, her silver hair in a pixie cut. She seems elegant, and it's clear how happy she is to see Jack.

"Now I know where Jack gets his big blue eyes." This is one of the first things I say to her, but my words come out weakly, not sounding like me at all, timid or perhaps soft-spoken, which would be my best hope versus plain, old, horribly, stupidly hungover. My first minutes at the table are spent in a perma-smile as I fixate on the floral centerpiece and will myself not to vomit.

Julia's ninety-two-year-old husband is also there, Jack's stepfather, Nicholas. Born and raised in France, Nicholas immigrated to the United States to study at Yale, where he met Jack's father. The two men seemed fated to be best friends for a lifetime. Until . . .

Jack has told me this whole story before now, but in my swimmy, booze-addled state, it all comes flooding back. Twenty years ago, Jack's father learned that Nicholas has been carrying on an affair with Julia most of their married life. The news broke him to the point that he even begged Julia to stay married, Nicholas or not. They divorced, and Jack's father died, heartbroken, after a lengthy battle with brain cancer.

So there is that elephant on this lovely porch in summertime Nantucket. I watch Jack converse with Nicholas, looking for hints that might reveal his true feelings for the man, but I can detect only ease, even fondness. Is this forgiveness, or simply impeccable manners?

Nicholas, Julia, and Jack are laughing. These people see each other every week and Jack seems easy here, committed to caring for both of them. They're a family, aren't they? Julia betrayed Jack's father. Jack, too. How much has this colored his view of women, his ability to commit?

My nausea subsides and the food begins to perk me up. I tease Jack for reading his emails on his phone during lunch and Julia and Nicholas nag along with me. We are having a little fun. I feel like this meeting has gone well.

When lunch is finished, Jack and I help his parents home. "I like your sandals,"

Julia says, smiling at my feet as we wait for the taxi. I thank her. I agonized over what to wear today.

We deliver Julia and Nicholas to their oceanside Tudor-style home. Everyone squeezes out of the taxi again to say our goodbyes. Nicholas takes both my hands in his, saying, "I hope we will see you again."

"I hope so, too," I say.

Jack and I watch as Nicholas takes Julia's bag and tucks it under his arm, his hand at the small of her back as she negotiates the walker toward their front door. I wonder what Jack is thinking in this moment. Maybe that it should be his own father at this mother's side, the way I once did, watching Gary, my stepfather, with my mother, imagining what life might be like if my mother and my real father were still together.

In the taxi barreling back to the hotel, Jack takes my hand. He waits until I meet his eyes. "Thank you," he says.

"Of course." I feel like this meant something to him.

Later that afternoon, under the cool sheets of the hotel bed, I will lose myself. "I love you," I will say to Jack and, in return, he will say nothing.

♥

Date #35: The Natural Course

Over breakfast, Jack mentions that his mother called last night. "She said that you were very classy."

"Classy?" I burst out laughing.

"Sure fooled her," Jack says.

I cover my face with my hands, remembering my dire condition.

I study him for a moment. "You know, meeting your mother and stepfather has got me thinking."

"What's that?"

"I guess seeing all that you've gone through—all of you—and yet we were able to have a lunch like we did yesterday."

"Yes."

"And your mother and Nicholas have such a vulnerability, a fragility at their age. It makes me think of my father. That he is getting on in his years and he won't be around much longer. I mean, maybe I should find him. I don't know for sure if he's even still alive."

Jack nods. "Look at what happened to my father. He's gone now."

"Even after everything . . ."

"He is your *father*," Jack says.

"It's overwhelming." A lump is forming in my throat.

Jack locks eyes with me. "What are you—*chicken*?"

"Chicken?"

"Yeah, chicken. Are you?"

I stare down at a piece of toast.

"It's the natural course of things. To know your parents," Jack says.

I pick up my fork and push the food on my plate in circles and wonder how this discussion has even come about. I started this. "It's not easy. I've told you. He abandoned three families."

"There could be more to the story than you realize," Jack says. He has never talked to me like this before. With such conviction.

I stare back at him for a moment. "Fine. I will think about it," I say, wondering how there might be more to the story when there's a legal transcript with my father questioning paternity of Margot and me. My mother is a lot of things, but I'm quite sure she deeply loved my father and didn't cheat on him.

Later that afternoon, Jack and I sit in white Adirondack chairs overlooking the ocean. Our last moments together are often by the water. His flight to Boston departs a few hours before mine so I will stay in town. When he leaves, once again, there is no discussion of when we might see each other again. I watch him walk away across the lawn, his long, tall frame, the easy gait, his head slightly bent.

But now I've met his mother. That's something, isn't it?

♥

CHAPTER 16

A Game of Chicken

Chicken. That word, Jack's insinuation—or was it a challenge—has been going through my head the last two days since Nantucket. It's got me thinking hard about why it's struck a nerve. What are my fears? *There are very few things to be afraid of.* That had been my epiphany during the time of my tumor. When faced with nonexistence, fear falls away. I call Jack on the phone and he answers with a "*Mizzzz* Holly!" in a faux Southern accent.

"Oh, you're a Southern gentleman this evening?"

"I am indeed . . . from time-to-time," he drawls and I laugh. He tells me that he played golf this afternoon with an old friend from college.

"Nice. Know what I did yesterday?"

"*Do* tell . . ."

"Did a little digging, tracked down my father's sister, and in less than one hour, she and my uncle arranged a visit for me to see my father. I go mid-September. Don't know if I'm going to blame you or thank you," I say.

"You will thank me. It's the normal course of things."

"What?"

"To see your father—that's what's normal. It's the way it should be."

I sigh skeptically and tell him that I learned that my father has been having health problems recently, some arising from an accident three years ago when he was riding his bicycle and was hit by a car. "He's nearly eighty."

"I think this will be a positive experience for you," Jack says.

"I hope so. How's your mother doing?"

"The same."

"She's a sweetheart. Maybe she'll hang in there."

"No matter what rose-colored glasses you can try to put on, this is a bad situation," Jack says.

"Like one day you're just going to get a call?"

"Yes."

"I'm sorry." I swallow. "You know, we never talked about it, but why did you want me to meet her?" My pulse quickens.

"Well, Mother has a home in Nantucket, as you know," Jack says. His lighthearted tone has disappeared and he's choosing his words carefully. "You and I were there on the island. I went through various scenarios. Not go see her, go see her without you, or go and say it doesn't mean anything. In the end, I decided to just not address it."

"You never gave me a context."

"Point taken," Jack says, and then oddly he moves to talking about what he calls our "geography issue." This is the first I've ever heard his thoughts on the subject. "I can't move down there and you can't tell Evie that you're moving her to Boston." He's never even met Evie. Why? Because I don't entirely trust him.

"I guess it depends on whether you value quality or convenience," I say.

"I don't even know what to say to that," Jack says. The tone of his voice has become the slightest bit of angry.

Neither one of us speaks for a minute and then I say, "There are ways of making it work, but if you view it as a major issue, then I guess it is. I realize that we've known each other since March and I don't know what you're looking for. Do you want to date casually or do you want a relationship?"

"I had told you that I didn't know."

"That's becoming more problematic for me." I pause, thinking of the right words. "Because . . . because now I do know what I want."

"I know I need to figure that out."

"Well if you do figure it out, come find me."

"We'll talk again," Jack says, the words beginning as a statement but with the edge of concern that perhaps it's open to question.

"If after forty-five years I can sort out my father, surely I can sort out Jack Carver!" Jack chuckles a little but I'm also sensing his realization of a shift. I'm becoming less chicken to ask the tough questions. "When we're together, you and I reveal a lot to each other—very personal things. We can talk about everything except us," I say.

"There's some truth in that," Jack says.

"Are you seeing other people?"

"No. I don't know why."

"I am. No one I'm really crazy about, but I guess my instincts about you were right," I say.

"You're right—I owe you more clarity," Jack says.

"C'mon. At our age, we only get so many more times at bat."

"You're right. Life is short. I need to figure this out not only for you, but also for me."

We wish each other a good night and when our call is over, I lie in bed a while, unable to sleep, thinking of how we're approaching a fork in the road. Apparently, my fears were justified: Jack doesn't know what he wants, and my meeting his mother didn't mean a damn thing. And if it didn't mean a thing, then I must not mean much to him, either. How can I think otherwise? I'm in love with a man who doesn't love me.

♥

Date #36: Devil Dog

Fletcher with the crew cut and weathered face is a former Marine originally from Texas. We meet up for a first date in a wine bar. Now working in "private equity," he frequently travels to Iraq, Jordan, Afghanistan, Venezuela, Chile—some badass places. His travels and connections have me wondering what he actually does do for a living; he seems a kind of Marlborough Man/James Bond. Though his profile says he's a non-smoker, he smells distinctly of cigarettes. At six-foot-four, he looks like he can handle himself in any situation and there's an intensity, bordering on ferocity, to Fletch.

He's got three kids and says he met his wife on a blind date when he was twenty-six and she was nineteen. "At nineteen, my wife was more mature than me. After three weeks, I knew she would be the mother of my children," he says.

They had a good run of happiness for a time. "Seven years ago, she told me I needed to move to my own bedroom," he says. Fletch adds that his in-laws were both psychologists and that separate bedrooms was their arrangement, too, so his wife grew up thinking this was normal.

I ask Fletch who initiated his divorce. "I did," he answers. "She stared at the divorce papers in disbelief when I handed them to her. She thought the no-sex thing wouldn't be a problem."

We finish our wine and the hour we've spent together was certainly interesting enough. Fletch walks me to my car. It's early on a Sunday evening and the air is warm and filled with noise from nearby restaurants, laughter, people out enjoying the dimming summer sunshine. At my car, Fletch bends to kiss me on the lips just as I go to kiss his cheek, and we collide in an awkward hybrid of a half-kiss with saliva and sore noses. I laugh and give him a hug instead.

"I've had a great time. Will you go out with me again?" Fletch says.

I look up at him. "I don't know." *Or do I?* He looks a little disappointed and then I give him another hug.

"Get home safe, sweetie," he says.

In the car, I see he's already texted me, asking again. *I'll sleep on it. Still hesitating.*

The next day, I will hear from him again asking the same question. "Can we go out again?"

I decline. There's something that just makes me uneasy about him. I cannot put my finger on it. And after I send my gently worded text saying that I enjoyed meeting him but don't think a second date makes sense, he replies: "You have a high opinion of yourself. Why do you think it's okay to waste my time?"

Wow. Gentle to psycho. Trust your gut for sure.

♥

Back in California, solo. Evie is with David on vacation for two weeks. Jack calls early one evening.

He's sitting outside on his deck and I tell him I'm outside, too, on my patio, getting a little late afternoon sun. From Boston comes the sounds of Jimmy Buffett playing an outdoor concert, the music echoing across the water. "*Wasted away again in Margaritaville . . . some people claim that there's a woman to blame . . .*" Jack sings to me. I laugh half-heartedly. Is there any significance to these lyrics or to anything that happens between us?

I try to keep things light and tell him a story about a husband and wife, both dentists who befriended Evie and me in a restaurant, and how they secretly smuggled Evie a jawbreaker the size of a baseball.

I ask about his mother. She's the same. Jack repeats that she and Nicholas think I'm very "classy."

"Did you tell her that she doesn't know me?" I say.

"Yeah, I've got some pictures," Jack says.

Then somehow we move to a discussion of us. "You know, we should probably communicate more," I say.

"I'm a guy!" Jack says. "I'm not good at it."

"At least we know you're straight."

"That I am," Jack says, laughing. "I've been thinking about it. I realize that I'm self-protecting."

"What are you protecting against?"

"Uhh." Jack clears his throat. "Getting hurt. And I suppose I'm trying to protect my time and freedom."

"Okay. Well, if you're saying the long-distance is a deal breaker . . .?"

"It's not a deal breaker," Jack says firmly. "I just don't know if I want a relationship or to casually date. I need time."

"Okay." I am taking in his words, the words I don't want to hear.

"I don't know what will make me happy," Jack says. "I asked one of my board members the other day how to be happy, and the board member says you simply do the opposite of what makes you unhappy."

"Have you considered that it's love that might bring happiness?"

"It has. For short periods of time."

"Given what I've gone through, I know it's the only thing that matters." I pause. "Maybe you're overthinking it."

"I overthink everything," Jack says.

I sigh. "We have that in common. Is this about you still getting over a fourteen-year relationship?"

"I don't know if I'll ever be over it."

"Why?"

"Because it's not the way relationships should be," Jack answers, and now I'm baffled. What does he even mean? There have been some pauses in our conversation.

"I'm just digesting everything," I say, finally. "I guess I need to think about if this is something I can live with," but already, deep down, I know the answer.

"I'm going to go now," Jack says sternly. He has decreed the conversation to be over.

After, I sit and cry for a bit. I'm crying because the reality is that Jack isn't the man I hoped he'd be. And I've fallen in love with him.

I dry my tears and take a breath and remind myself that I just have to stay the course. What other choice do I have? I'm not giving up. I need to keep dating other people and living my own life and will hang in there with Jack as long as I can stand it, in the hopes that maybe someday his feelings will match mine for him. And in the meantime, maybe I will meet someone better, someone who knows what he wants, who values himself and me. Dating is a marathon. Run, don't stop, that's all you have to do.

My phone rings again. This time it's my sister, Margot. "What's wrong?" she says, somehow just knowing. "Aww," she soothes. "Do you have a picture of him? I need to put a face with a name."

I text her a headshot from Jack's corporate website; he's in a suit and tie, looking directly into the camera. Confident, the leader, with the slightest suggestion of a smile.

"Hmm . . ." Margot says.

"What?"

"You will never be the apple of that man's eye," she says, sighing.

"You think?"

"Yeah. You can tell a lot about a man by looking into his eyes. You need more than this, Holly."

Her words sting. Margot is usually right.

♥

Date #37: Consenting Adults

There's a firefighter shortage. Wildfires are burning to the north, and there's a strain on resources. Graham has been mandated to work for several days with no end in sight. That means no dates for the foreseeable future, till the smoke clears, literally. It's almost like dating the incarcerated. But then Graham has the idea that I pay him a visit tonight after everyone has gone to sleep. Does breaking into a firehouse count as a date? Maybe I'm losing my mind.

At first, I'd dismissed the idea as a joke, but he persisted, with no less than thirty texts, two phone calls, and photos from the first night we met. *Why not? We're two consenting adults*. And technically, I'm not breaking in, I'm sneaking in. Quietly. "Who are we hurting?" Graham asked.

"No one, I guess." Still unconvinced.

It's after 11:00, and I wait in a bar two blocks from the station as he texts me updates. The guys are all in the rec room right off the kitchen. I can picture it clearly—the semicircle of leather recliners around the enormous flat screen. One by one, like a reverse game of musical chairs, they're slowly taking their leave. I picture them yawning, glancing up at the wall clock, saying there's nothing worth watching on TV anyway, each one saying his good night before wandering off to bed with the same hope as every night—no calls and a full night's sleep.

But it's taking a hell of a long time for them to turn in. And the longer I wait, the more nervous I become, the longer I second-guess myself and what I'm about to do. Maybe it'll be just a few stolen kisses or some quiet conversation? C'mon, Holly, really?

I think of Jack and wonder what he's up to right now, if he's alone. I've hardly heard from him since our last conversation. It's as though he's angry with me for wanting to understand why we're dating, where he's coming from. *Screw you, Jack.*

I order another drink and check my phone. Not yet. Just what the hell am I doing? *Am I doing this to spite him?* I'm flattering myself. Jack wouldn't even care, which hurts more.

In our texting back and forth today, Graham and I weighed the risks. This is more of a smuggling operation, but it's verboten, of course, and what if we get caught? "Could you lose your job?" was one of the first things I asked.

"Probably not," Graham answered.

"What if there's a fire?" Do I just hide in his room till the fire trucks leave and then I sneak away? What if all the doors lock and I can't get out? I picture myself cowering in the janitor's closet with the mop, or sliding down the fire pole, half-clad, trying to run for the nearest exit.

And what about security cameras? There has to be a million cameras everywhere. What if I get arrested for being in the firehouse when I'm not supposed to be? What if I end up on the six o'clock news?

I've seen for myself that Graham has his own room. But what he hasn't told me yet is that it's right next door to the Captain's.

I am the mother of a darling, perceptive girl who looks up to me. Respectability is essential to parenthood. Just who am I to me versus my responsibility to her? Why does society struggle with the idea of mothers as sexual beings? Why do I struggle with that notion myself?

As I wait, I think more about Graham. My God, he's single, I'm single. We are indeed consenting adults. Who *are* we hurting here?

I think about my attraction to him and our spark and, frankly, just how damn good-looking, how damn nice, so earnest and sweet and strong. His muscular body, his smooth, coffee-colored skin, his physical perfection. A hot, thirty-three-year-old fireman. Like this will ever happen again?

I think about how my entire life, I have mostly done all the "right" things, how I was taught to be ashamed of my body and sex, to live in fear, that "nice" girls don't like sex or at least they deny that desire within themselves. I reflect on my two failed marriages and the disappointment and scant affection. I realize how stifled I feel in my uptight, Connecticut life, but how this moment makes me feel alive again. Meeting Graham is completely unplanned, off-script—this isn't part of the typical middle-aged stay-at-home mother-homemaker program. For the first time in a very long while, I feel like the -eighteen-year-old girl who bought a one-way ticket to Tel Aviv and began life as an adventure. It's time I got that girl back.

I think, too, about regret. I wonder if, as an old woman, when I look back on this moment, will I regret this?

I decide that I'm more likely to regret *not* doing this.

I remember that morning in Boston, the day after the diagnosis at Dana Farber, staring out my window in stunned disbelief, watching people walking by, going about their lives, believing that they have years and years ahead. *That was me yesterday,* I'd thought. And now I'm still here. Shouldn't I live now, more than ever?

I've always been such a Miss Goody Two-Shoes, a nerd, a geek. "Polly Purebred" as a male coworker once taunted me; I'm so boringly, predictably responsible.

Damn it, I'm going in.

♥

Graham texts that the coast is clear.

We meet at the back of the station, and in the dim light, I see him in his uniform in the blue shirt, keying in the code to open an electronic gate. Silently, he motions for me to stand off to the side in the shadows, away from the glare of a floodlight. We watch the gate slowly open. Wordlessly, Graham walks through and takes my hand and motions for me to follow, carefully hugging the building's perimeter. He points up to a camera. Now I understand—this way, we will not be recorded on video.

We wait for the gate to close again. *I'm locked in.* The sound of the creaking metal seems just too loud—won't this wake someone?

We stand perfectly still for a few seconds, listening. All quiet.

Slowly, he opens a door and we step inside. It is almost completely dark, and I can see nearly nothing but for the outline of fire trucks and some light filtering in on the staircase that leads to the upper level and Graham's room.

But Graham guides me in a different direction, away from the staircase.

"Are we going to your room?" I whisper.

"We can't. The Captain's room is next door to mine."

"What?"

"Shh . . . this way."

Through the dark, he leads me to another place. I hear a key in a lock, the opening of a door. He pops a light switch for a split second, and fluorescent light briefly floods the room and then he flicks it off again. We're in what looks like a conference room.

"I brought us blankets and pillows," he whispers, kneeling down on the floor, showing me with the flashlight on his phone. In the corner, behind the table, he has made us a bed, a cozy little nest. Propped in the corner is a radio.

"Why the radio?"

"I have to listen for calls."

I take a deep breath. "Right. And what if there is one?"

"Just stay here."

"Okay." *I cannot believe I'm doing this.*

"And don't worry," he whispers, finding my hand in the dark. He presses a square packet into my palm. "I brought these." A condom.

"You are the original Boy Scout," I say, laughing softly. "Thank you." He gently squeezes my shoulders and then kisses me.

We are both nervous, and there are bumps and misses, the hitting of a tooth as we try to find each in the dark. His lips are so full and soft and he takes his time when he kisses me. This man knows what he's doing. Then he pulls away. "This is my first time," he says solemnly.

I just about stop breathing. "Wait. You're a virgin?"

"No. My first time in the station."

"Oh my God!" Now I am silently shaking with laughter, trying not to make any noise. "My God! You scared me."

"Sorry . . ." Graham laughs a little, too.

"Well, I hope you don't do this every day, because I can tell you that I sure don't . . ." We are kissing again and the moment has helped ease our nerves.

We crawl beneath the blankets and find each other. I'm beginning to almost, almost, forget where we. Our clothes are coming off, and Graham is proving to be a generous lover. Small, unexpected kisses, a caressing of my hair and concern that I'm okay and enjoying myself, as though from a man I've known a very long time.

Suddenly, there is a crack on the radio and the voice of a dispatcher pierces the quiet. We freeze. "Shhh," Graham says. "Listen for the code." From what I can tell, it's a medical emergency. Graham and his partner are the two firefighters trained to respond to most medical emergencies. I cannot make out everything the dispatcher says, but then I hear "Code 3."

Graham exhales audibly. "Okay." He kisses me again. "Code 3 is a non-emergency. I can stay."

I flop onto the floor and bury my face in the pillow. "Oh my God!" I say into it. "I thought . . ."

Graham is kissing me again.

Later, in the dark, he helps me dress and steal away. The gate opens again and we have one last, quick kiss. I begin walking quickly, my heart pounding, and I hear the gate closing behind. I turn back and see Graham in the shadows, and he raises his hand in a wave and I blow him a kiss good night. Then I break into a run.

♥

CHAPTER 17

Smoke Signals

Date #38: Here's to You, Ann Bancroft

Jack can stew in his juices, contemplate his navel, stay tangled in his mental underwear—I need to get on with my life, not fixate on a man who doesn't know what he wants at sixty. Every time I think of Graham, I can't stop smiling. He's such an unexpected, wonderful delight.

Graham arrives at my house in the early evening a few days after our firehouse encounter. I have zero regrets. In the light of dusk, from my kitchen window, I can see his white pickup truck pull into the driveway. The day has been hot, and he's driven with the windows down. He jumps out bare-chested and stretches a black T-shirt over his ripped shoulders, striding up the front steps. I want to ask him if he always drives with his shirt off, but I don't. I open the door and he's standing there and we smile a little awkwardly at each other. He's all long and lanky with radiant, dark skin. *Youth.*

"Come in," I say a little stiffly, immediately regretting how it sounds. It seems to make all of this too formal somehow, and I sound a little patrician, like some kind of Mrs. Robinson. Why can't I stop thinking of that damn movie?

In the kitchen, I offer him a drink and he chooses champagne and then, flutes in hand, I give him a tour of my house, which feels empty and too quiet with Evie away.

But if Evie were here, of course, Graham wouldn't be, and it's exciting to be alone together. Finally, we have time and privacy.

In bed later, in the light of flickering candles and dancing shadows, Graham and I laze under the sheets, curled together, talking quietly. We tell each other where we grew up, went to college, about our families.

He attended college in the Midwest on a basketball scholarship. He missed the NBA, but one of his best friends made it in. He was a good student but sports were always his favorite.

Graham's father, a strapping, six-foot-four man, was born and raised in Sierra Leone and immigrated to the United States in his early twenties. His mother, Costa Rican and petite, worked as a legal secretary to support Graham and his sister after

Graham's father left his mother for another woman. His father remarried and Graham has three half-siblings.

"My father left us, too," I say.

"Mom worked hard to raise us as a single mother. Raised us Catholic."

"Are you religious?"

"Not at all. But Mom still is." Graham tells me that he puts in overtime so he can send money to help her and that he's saving for a down payment on a first house.

I wonder about his day-to-day life as a firefighter. "Tell me about a call you went on this week?"

He thinks for a second. "There was a woman who passed out at the wheel, sheared off a fire hydrant, and drove into someone's house."

"Oh no. And then you show up on the scene."

"Yeah. We fix it. Preserve life and property."

"Such important work."

"I like what I do," Graham says with conviction, and I can tell that it's true. He's got a sense of purpose, and my mind drifts to Jack. Unlike Jack, Graham seems happy.

I ask him how he deals with death, the tragedies? The horrible car accidents and the like.

"With older people, it's easier. They've lived. It's the kids, the teenagers . . ."

"I don't know how you handle it."

"We call them 1144s," Graham says.

"1144s?"

"That's the code for a fatality."

"Oh. Like a Code 3," I say, remembering the night at the firehouse, still not quite believing that actually happened or that this beautiful man is here in my bed.

"It can be hard. But people are born every day and they die every day, too."

"You seem accepting of it."

Graham shrugs. "I never forget their faces, though."

"God." I roll over and kiss his cheek. This Graham is young in years, yet rich in wisdom. This is a man, not a boy. A real adult.

He tells me about his younger sister and their pact. She's a police officer in San Francisco and their mother worries constantly about them both. The deal is that whenever his mom asks either of them about work, the answer is always the same: "It's slow."

Graham gets out of bed. He's naked, and I can't help but marvel at him again as I watch him move through my bedroom, stooping to blow out the candles. *We wouldn't want a fire.* He comes back to bed and we hold each other, drifting off to sleep, till morning.

♥

Date #39: Tell the Whole Truth

There won't be a Vegas wedding. Ryan, the baseball-cap-wearing-comedian who calls me Yeti, has sent me a text summing up the result of our last date:

> We tell the whole truth to each other, right? So say it. Even in its simplest form. Text it even. "You're going to disappear." It's ok . . . but say it. Send smoke signals, say it.

And I will. I'll tell him the truth: that I don't feel the big feelings necessary to go forward. And that we both know the whole "let's be friends" thing is nearly impossible when one cares more than the other. The admission is difficult for us both.

And so here I am, still trying to patch it together. If only I could combine Ryan's openheartedness and passion with the things that I admire in Jack, like his intellect, wit, and sexiness, along with Graham's courage, wisdom, selflessness, physical perfection. Seems impossible to find it all in just one man.

♥

CHAPTER 18

A Welcome Home

I'm leaving California early for an important reason: to close on my new house in Connecticut. I'm thrilled. I've been in a holding pattern for too long.

Legal documents exchanged, funds transferred, and I drive to my real estate attorney's office. It's a little past 8:00 a.m. and everything has gone smoothly. My attorney hands over keys and closing documents.

Walking up the front path to my new house, I notice the garden is blooming with pink roses and enormous blue hydrangeas, shaded by a canopy of trees. I slide the key into the lock and open the door.

My steps echo on hardwood floors. The house is empty and move-in ready, the previous owners retired to Florida.

I stand in the kitchen, looking around, touching countertops and opening cupboards, then wandering through each room, imagining our new life here . . . and I begin to cry. *I did it.* I think about everything that has brought me to this moment, for what feels like a very long journey.

My phone is ringing. "I'm standing here in my new house. I'm actually a little emotional . . ."

"Congratulations," Jack says. "Now tell me again what train you're on? I'll pick you up at the station."

♥

Date #40: Just Drop It

A hot summer weekend in Boston. The afternoon is sticky when Jack picks me up, a fine glow of perspiration across his upper lip as we kiss. Just as I get in his car, my phone rings so I pull it out of my handbag. In full view, we can both see that it's someone named Alton calling. I turn beet red, decline the call, and dump the phone back in my bag like a hot potato. Jack laughs. "Is that another one of your men?" he says.

While I'm embarrassed, another part of me is glad that Jack knows that I haven't entirely been sitting home alone pining for him.

♥

Date #41: Bard Wager

Saturday morning, we have lunch with a group of Jack's friends at a waterside restaurant in the shade of patio umbrellas. They are all in their early sixties like him, their wives around the same age. It might be my imagination, but the wives seem a little frosty. Jack is sixteen years my senior, almost old enough to be my father.

Later that afternoon, I go for a run before dinner, and when I return, I take a shower. It's the inaugural shower in Jack's newly renovated bathroom, the harbor-facing wall entirely made of glass. "I think I'm giving some boaters a show," I call to Jack, who is nearby, watching TV and reading.

"Excellent," Jack says. I come out of the bathroom wrapped in a towel and look down at him in his recliner, in a white bathrobe and reading glasses, his book open in his lap, and I kiss the top of his head. Suddenly I'm overcome with a feeling that I could do this everyday life stuff with him, always. I go to the mirror and put on my makeup, and we call to each other as I'm getting ready.

For dinner, Jack takes me to a romantic French restaurant, and we sit side-by-side in the banquette, my head on his shoulder. We eat oysters and rare steaks and drink cold martinis, and when we get back to his house, we go skinnydipping. Standing on the edge of the pool, I am struck by how good this feels. And it's not that I'm naked, or silly, or drunk on a summer evening. I'm happy. And it doesn't matter that my mother once said I walked funny or my ex-husband is my second ex-husband. I'm free.

In the water, we splash and flirt, our limbs intertwining, and then somehow, he says something about the witches in Hamlet.

I snort. "There are no witches in *Hamlet*."

"There are witches in *Hamlet*," Jack says firmly.

"There are ghosts in *Hamlet*, witches in *Macbeth*," I answer, even more firmly.

"No. Witches in *Hamlet*," Jack says.

"Really? You want to bet an English major on this?"

"You're on," Jack says.

We shake hands through the water. "A thousand bucks. A thousand bucks no witches in *Hamlet*. Ghosts in *Hamlet*. Witches in *Macbeth*."

"Easiest thousand bucks I've ever made!" he says.

We jump out of the pool and begin running, buck naked, back to Jack's house.

Still dripping wet, I sprint to the third floor and find my phone. We collapse on his bed laughing and horsing around. I Google the question. "Look at this! Look at this!" I yell, handing him my phone. "Read it aloud, baby . . ."

Jack takes my phone. "The three witches in Shakespeare's *Macbeth* . . ." he reads aloud.

"I want my money!"

"Punk!" Jack says.

Eventually, we tire each other out and I fall asleep in his arms.

♥

Date #42: Elusive Rest

Sunday morning, we awake, lazing in bed, listening to the heavy rain that rolled in overnight. "How'd you sleep?" I ask, wrapped around him.

"Not well. You didn't hear me get up?"

"No. Slept like a baby."

"I woke up and heard the rain so I got up to bring in the pillows and patio cushions."

"Didn't hear a thing."

"I don't know why I'm so neurotic about it. They're just cushions."

"Sorry you didn't sleep well," I say, but really, they are just cushions. Why can't you ever be at rest?

♥

Date #43: Sweetheart Victor

The same night I return from Boston, I decide, last second, to have a drink with a guy I've been trying to schedule with for awhile. Why? Because, as usual, I left Boston today with nothing resolved with Jack and no plans to see each other again.

This suitor is a lawyer by the name of Victor, and I discover he's a truly nice man—warm, genuine, ready for a relationship, but dammit, I'm just not into him. I wish it were otherwise. I spend an hour with him and then ease my way out the door.

One foot in front of the other, like a marathon. Just keep going.

Crazy busy day tomorrow. Moving day. Sleep. I need sleep.

♥

The next morning, another text from persistent Victor. Finally, in between packing boxes and directing movers, I answer:

> Vic, I feel bad but know that I have to be honest & upfront about my feelings. I'm open to a friendship as I think you're a terrific person but I think we lack the requisite spark romantically.
>
> **Victor**: No reason to feel bad about being honest.

The man has a point. Don't feel bad about being honest. And then he continues:

> I'm open to a friendship too as I think you're a really terrific person. I'm curious about your reservations about me . . . please be brutally honest as to why you were so quick to make a decision about me. If I offended you in any way, I am sorry.
>
> **Me**: You're a perfect gentleman! I think it's just a chemistry thing. Hard to know why but nonetheless I think we'd be great friends.
>
> **Victor**: Looking forward to that, neighbor. But I have to warn you that you will want to love me if you hang with me! I am very physically attracted to you and quite willing to surprise you in that department.

Surprises in that department. If I offended you in any way. So awkward. Will this ever get any easier?

♥

CHAPTER 19

The Things We Do for Love

Date #44: Move Over Hamilton & Burr

Alton Manley might be a time traveler. He's the only guy I've dated/not-dated who's challenged someone to a duel. The duel—or shall I say the *alleged* duel—took place on a Caribbean island where Alton served as ambassador and involved the dastardly brother of an iconic female fashion designer. Word got back to Washington and they had to intervene. But I digress.

When I say dated/not-dated, it's because I've told Alton that my heart belongs to someone who lives in Boston, but if Alton is willing to settle for companionship, I'm happy to be his friend. Alton loves the theater, like me, and he's looking for someone to join him at the local playhouse where he's got season tickets. Sounds harmless enough.

I'd met Alton a few weeks earlier at the Spotted Horse Tavern where I was eating dinner at the bar, and Alton had literally inserted himself between me and another man. Alton barged in, ordered a drink, and started a conversation, turning his back to the other guy. Barrel-chested with a round face and rosacea, I didn't find myself attracted to Alton, though he did strike me as a character.

Within a minute or two, we were chatting about England. He spends a significant amount of time there since his company, of which he is the Grand Poobah, is headquartered in the United Kingdom. That detail seemed to explain Alton's funky fusion of American and British accents, but I couldn't tell if it was affected or legit. He'd steered the conversation toward anecdotes of his regular interactions with members of the British royal family, descendants of Churchill, etcetera. Quirky and captivating, but alas, Alton is not hot. He handed me his card, which I politely accepted, and then he promptly departed. I returned to my conversation with the other guy, an amiable plumber who rides Harleys on weekends.

A good ten minutes later, when Alton was all but forgotten and plumberman was mid-sentence, telling a good story, Alton returned. Plumberman and I clam up and there was an awkward still. Alton looked back and forth between us before turning to me. "I just wanted to give you this," he said, handing me another one of his business cards.

"Oh. You gave me one already. Remember?" And I began to wonder if Alton might have dementia.

"But I've written something on this one," he said, flipping it over. In flowing, feminine script, Alton has transcribed a quote:

> "It is only with the heart that one can see rightly, what is essential is invisible to the eye." —Antoine de Saint-Exupéry

"One of my favorite quotes," Alton said. "I know you'd appreciate it."

"Wow," I said, staring down at the card. "You have such nice . . . penmanship."

"It's because I only write with fountain pens!" Alton said, and behind him, I thought I heard the plumber snickering. "I look forward to hearing from you, Holly," Alton said, dramatically, turning on his heel and taking his leave a second time through the front door.

The next day, I emailed Alton—I admit, I was curious about him. He was just so unusual and over-the-top, but I was also touched by the sensitivity and vulnerability of not only the quote but his approach. The idea of seeing through the heart. Doesn't it take courage to lead with that sentiment, especially in a bar?

In my email to Alton, I explained that it was nice to have met him, I appreciated the gesture, but that I was already seeing someone. From there, we landed at an agreement that we both love theater and are single, it's no fun going to the theater alone, we live near each other too, so let's be friends and theater buddies.

The night of the theater date/non-date, Alton offers to pick me up, but I politely decline. No way. A woman needs her own wheels, especially when she's out with someone she doesn't know well.

Alton suggests that we meet for dinner beforehand at a French restaurant, not far from the playhouse.

When I arrive, Alton is dressed in a navy blazer and cotton pants the color of boiled lobsters. He hands me a bouquet of a dozen white roses, the stems trellised in satin ribbon. These aren't ratty roses picked up from the corner deli; these are expensive, from a fancy floral designer, and when I see them, my spirits sink. He has either forgotten or is deliberately ignoring our friendship pact.

The French restaurant is romantic, by the water, he knows the owner, who has given us the best table. Another bad sign. This all screams DATE.

Later, in the theater, as we're watching the performance, I sense Alton fumbling around in the dark. Sure enough, his hand is near my thigh and he finds my hand and takes it in his.

I sit there for a second, feeling my hand in his, my palm growing clammy, and all I can think is *now what? Maybe I'm just too polite. I don't want to make a scene. The drama should be up there on stage, not here.*

I give it another minute or so and then slowly I withdraw my hand, as casually as possible, crossing my arms across my chest.

The remainder of the evening goes fine. We both pretend the hand-holding incident never happened, and we talk about the play, which happens to be *The Things We Do for Love*. Indeed.

♥

Date #45: Humorous Heath

Freckle-faced Heath, who I met online, has a sense of humor. He just laughs when I show up late for our dinner date almost still dripping wet from the shower. "At least I'm not as bad as my friend, Rose," I say.

"How's that?"

"When Rose doesn't have time to shower, she just douses her clothes in Febreze." Heath cracks up. He laughs so easily that it makes him immensely likable.

He's a high school teacher at a private school, two hours away. Undeterred by lengthy time in the car, he's offered to make the trek to my town. Nice-looking in a boyish sort of way, he appears a decade younger than me even though we're about the same age.

Heath knows the principal of Evie's school; he grew up nearby and we know some of the same people. A trust quickly builds.

Heath's son, Gavin, is a year younger than Evie. "We spend a lot of time on the water," Heath says. "I have a sailboat and Gavin loves to sleep outside on deck."

"Being rocked to sleep by the waves is the best."

"Maybe you and Evie can join us sometime," Heath says.

"That would be fun."

The hint of a future meeting with our children. An auspicious start.

♥

Date #46: Turn Down the TV

The last heavy heat of August lingers, and everyone and every thing moves in slow motion as the air conditioners drone on. Heath calls. He sounds so cheerful, he's practically exuberant. "I don't normally ask this since we've only gone out once—but would you and Evie like to go ziplining with me and Garth this weekend?"

"Ziplining? We've never tried that." The typical summer activities have been exhausted: day camps, the beach, museums and parks.

"It's really a play date, isn't it, if we have the kids?" Heath says.

"I'm a little afraid of heights . . ."

"It'll be fun!" Heath says.

"We'd love to join you." *Well, Evie would love to join you.* I give Evie the straight scoop—that I've gone out once with Heath, the jury is still out on him, but he seems very nice and this is an opportunity to try ziplining with another kid. She's excited.

First impressions of Heath's son, Garth, are positive, and he and Evie seem to get along. The boy is small for his age with wheat-blonde hair, and while he doesn't say a lot, when he does, it's thoughtful.

Heath looks different than the other night. He's wearing cargo shorts and a baseball cap, carting a backpack full of water and snacks for everyone. The man plans ahead. "Listen up!" Heath says. "The park needs us to take a safety lesson first." *He is talking to the kids in a different voice. The voice is slower, more deliberate, with simple words, ver-y clear-ly e-nun-ci-ated. Heath has Teacher Voice!* But the kids don't even notice, they just respond.

The remainder of the afternoon, Heath leads the charge, talking in that voice. The man is in his element, confident, the ringleader, the mentor. The kids are having a blast. "Great job, Evie!" Heath yells as she flies off a high platform through the trees. "That's it, buddy! You've got this!" Heath calls in encouragement to his son. The kids screech in delight. I, on the other hand, am struggling with my fear of heights and my new aversion to Heath's Teacher Voice. Heath talks not only to the kids in TV, but me, too. "That's it, Hol-ly. You can do it, Hol-ly." It's becoming quite irritating.

From the moment I climb that first platform, I'm miserable. I've never liked heights, and even though I know that I'm technically safe, with the security of the tethers or whatever the hell it is that will catch me if I fall, I cannot overcome my love of good, solid earth. I keep looking down, feeling the distance between me and the ground. I gingerly make my way across the first two challenges. The first is like a tightrope, with handrails. My heart begins to pound, my legs tremble, and I struggle to keep my balance. I want to vomit. But I know what's coming. It's only going to get worse. *Breathe. Just breathe.* I have to zipline from a high platform, a great distance. Evie, the daredevil, has gone first, then Garth, then Heath. The three of them are watching me. Then a voice rings through the trees: "YOU NEED TO CONQUER YOUR FEAR!" It's Evie. My girl child is telling me to stare down my fear and do it anyway. I'm both mortified and proud. Nothing like having your own advice thrown back at you. Karma is a bitch.

I pause again. I look down at the ground. I take a deep breath. I squint through the trees to see Evie. I see Heath waving at me, smiling. Garth waits patiently. If this were the movies, I'd overcome my urge to cry and/or soil myself and show my daughter some moxie. I'd whiz through the trees upside down by one leg screaming the ziplining equivalent of "Suck my wake!"

What I do instead is plead to the park attendant: "CAN SOMEONE GET ME DOWN FROM HERE?"

I spend the rest of the afternoon at a picnic table licking my wounds while the voices of Teacher Man and happy children echo in the distance.

"You're so afraid of heights, Mom," Evie says, shaking her head as we are packing up to go.

"I'm sorry you didn't enjoy yourself," Heath says kindly.

"It's totally fine." I feel like a complete loser.

Later, after we've taken the kids to dinner and they've run ahead to buy ice cream, Heath will say, "We're finally alone."

"We are." A simple statement of a terrible fact. I'm ready to jump out of my skin. I'd even zipline outta here.

Heath kisses me on the lips, and I feel nothing other than wanting to wipe his saliva off my lips. Maybe gargle, too.

Heath calls me up and asks me out again a couple days later, and I politely decline. As gently as possible, I explain that I don't think we have the right mix of chemistry. He's a gentleman about it and seems to understand, but then a few days later, I receive an email from him. The email says that Heath spoke to his sister about me, and his sister asked if I knew that Heath has a really big cock. "No, she doesn't," Heath answered.

"You should tell her," says the sister.

Moreover, Heath's email goes on to say that every woman he's ever been with has multiple orgasms and that Heath has moves he knows I've never experienced before, and honestly, that his "cock feels so good it should be illegal." Do I want to come over for some "stargazing"?

"No, thank you," I answer and wish him and his beautiful boy all the best.

♥

Jack is in Montana over the Labor Day weekend, golfing with his buddies. He sends pictures of spectacular mountain scenery and videos of deer on the golf course. Sunday afternoon he texts that he's going for a hike by himself for a few hours. Late afternoon he texts again:

> Still on the mountain. Might have misjudged the distance. It's getting dark.
>
> **Me**: You okay?
>
> **Jack**: I think so.
>
> **Me**: Text when you're back safely. Stay in touch.

Another hour passes, and of course I begin to worry. No word and a number of scenarios play in my mind. If he's truly lost in the woods as night approaches, what should I do?

At an hour and a half, I hear back. He's found his way and all is well.

"So glad you're okay," I text. Relief. I await his response.

Nothing. It's as though he's fallen off the grid. I won't hear anything from him for another twenty-four hours, and when I finally do, he will say, "Just got your text. I appreciate the sentiment."

"Read" receipts, Jack. That was a day ago. But I say nothing. The lie speaks for itself.

♥

CHAPTER 20

Clouded Skies

Date #47: A Romantic Weekend

I've never been to Charleston, South Carolina.

Jack has heard me say to one of his friends that I've always wanted to go, and he's surprised me by suggesting that we meet up there. He has a conference during the week on Kiawah Island and then we'll meet up on Friday and stay the weekend together.

Charleston is a small city very connected with the water—two rivers merging with the Atlantic Ocean and wide, moody skies with ever-shifting clouds and dramatic light. Hot sun, then a sudden shower, and then the sun breaks through again. It's early September and the city is blanketed with a wet, heavy warmth.

Our hotel is in the heart of the historic district, old and quirky with whitewashed stone walls that block out the city's noise and heat. I've already checked in ahead of Jack when he texts that he's on his way.

Later, in the early evening, we take a pedi cab to dinner. We have a drink at the bar and Jack is more rested now and in the mood for flirtation and fun. We are called to be seated at our table.

The young waitress comes over, probably not a day over twenty-one. Perky and eager to please. "What brings you to Charleston?" she asks us, bright-eyed and earnest.

"Just a romantic weekend with my daughter," Jack says, deadpan. I nearly spit out my wine. Her face crumples to a look of alarm, and she stammers as she tries to recite the evening's specials. When she leaves the table, Jack and I burst out laughing.

"Did you really just say that?" I say, shaking my head.

"I did," Jack says, and he leans in to kiss me on the mouth as the waitress passes by the table.

"You're truly sick."

And it is. But it's also funny, and we laugh like we always do, all night long. It's hours later that I think Jack is almost old enough to be my father, and I wonder how that feels for him. And I know, too, that in every joke there is at least a grain of truth.

♥

Date #48: Black and Blue

We stroll along the Battery, a long, arching seawall with a view of Fort Sumter. The sky has shifted again, it's now black and blue and the wind has picked up. We walk together, enjoying the brisk breeze, when a young couple stops us and asks if we would take their picture. I do, then hesitate before asking, "Would you take ours?"

Somewhere in the back of my mind, I know it's crazy that I'm in love with a man I fear may not want his picture taken with me. Because it might mean we're a couple.

But Jack moves in at my side, his arm at my waist, and pulls me in. The photo is snapped, and later I will stare at it a long time, searching for clues, any sign, about us.

It's evening and we are going out to eat again. This Charleston weekend has been a food and wine extravaganza, trying some of the town's best restaurants. Tonight, it's McCrady's, housed in an old brick townhouse. We decide to eat at the bar, side-by-side, exactly like the first meal we shared together.

The cocktails and the wine begin to flow, and if I'd been more self aware, I'd know that something within me was beginning to break loose, too, like the cork being freed from our wine bottle, or the gates bursting on a dam. Maybe it was not one thing in particular, but a bunch of things—knowing that Jack and I have now been seeing each other for six months and we will be saying goodbye to each other again tomorrow and I still don't know where we stand. Maybe, without realizing it, I am deeply anxious about seeing my father in fewer than two weeks. Maybe I just feel that enough is enough.

"Every time I see you, I keep thinking this needs to be the last time," I say.

Jack looks shocked. "Why?"

My pulse quickens. "Because I don't know what we're doing here."

"We talk and text almost every day," Jack says, staring straight ahead.

"You've never asked me what I want," I say.

"Yes, I'm guilty of that."

"You cannot even acknowledge that we have a relationship."

Jack frowns. "We have a relationship," he says, taking a large sip of his wine.

"Now you're changing things on me. You can't even look at me, Jack."

Then he does look at me and stares deeply into my eyes. "You're right," he says. My chest has grown tight and I can feel tears welling up in my eyes. "Don't cry," Jack says gently.

I take a deep breath. "I won't cry."

I do cry.

Jack leans his face into mine and kisses my cheek. "Hey—it's okay." He rubs my back and then he puts his thumb in his mouth and waves his fingers at me. I burst out laughing through my tears.

"You can't do that! It's sacred!" I've told him that Evie has been doing that thumb-sucking wave at me since she was an infant. That she still does and it's our secret little code. But at least Jack has me laughing again.

I take a sip of water and clear my throat and try to compose myself. "I'm sorry. I don't know. Something is amiss. It seems that you live your life in a permanent hedge," I say.

"You're right." He takes another large sip of wine. "I have a hard time trusting anyone. Everyone has their agenda."

"Look at me." He meets my gaze and I meet him, eye to eye, with every ounce of openness I have, hoping he can feel my sincerity. "Of all the people—of all the women out there—am I not someone worth trusting?"

Jack stares intently into my eyes. "Yes," he says.

"I think we could be really happy together," I say. "We are happy together."

"Most people think I'm a happy person," Jack says.

"Are you?"

"Moments," Jack says.

"I don't care. I'm just going to say this. I love you and I'm in love with you. You don't need to say anything back."

There is silence. Jack doesn't look at me and my words hang out there. After a while, he says, "I'm not even sure if I want a girlfriend."

♥

I barely remember coming back to the hotel. I am falling apart. I start crying again. Jack and I are in bed together and I am crying. Primal sobbing that I haven't cried, as an adult, maybe ever. I'm going to lose Jack; he is not in love with me. This just doesn't feel right and it's destroying me. Jack is holding me and he's stroking my hair.

"I am so stupid. I don't know what I was thinking here . . ." I say, and I'm wailing again.

"You're smart."

"No, I'm not! I'm an utter fool."

"You're beautiful. I care for you deeply, Holly."

I am crying and he is kissing me and we are pulling off each other's clothes. He stops for a moment and asks very clearly if I am okay with this happening, that we will make love, and I say yes. And I am moved that he cared enough to ask and ensure the clarity of it. Maybe to be clear that he won't hurt me any more than he already has.

♥

Date #49: And You Let Her Go

Something terrible happened last night.

I slip out of bed. Jack is still sleeping. A trip to the bathroom to survey the damage in the harsh, fluorescent light. My eyelids are hard, swollen ridges. *I cried a lot last night.* I'm dizzy when I move my head. The night before is coming back to me in snippets and shadows. *I have ended things. I have ruined things. I have brought things to a head and Jack has told me the truth. His truth. I don't want to know his goddamn fucking truth.*

When I return, Jack is awake and he's sitting up in bed and this time it's me who can't look him in the eye. He has made me coffee on the little hotel coffeemaker, and we sit in bed together, staring straight ahead. He takes my free hand and holds it in his as I drink my coffee in silence.

"I knew you were going to break my heart," I say finally. Jack looks over at me like I've just slapped him. And now I've got more regret on top of the regret I'm already choking on. "I shouldn't have said that. I'm sorry," I say.

"I'm sorry I hurt you," Jack says. He stops. "No. I'm sorry you're hurting."

I look over at him and say nothing. *Thank you for your precise choice of words. Like we're on an earnings call with a tough question from a probing analyst. And now we have clarification from our CEO. Thank you, Mr. Carver. Mr. Carver will now take another question.*

"Can I help you?" Jack says.

"Just get me on the plane."

I get up and begin throwing clothes into my suitcase, storming around the room naked, everything hanging out and I do not care.

Jack watches. "I may be more uncompromising than Edwin," he says. Edwin is his brother. I stop in my tracks and stare wildly as he speaks. He talks about what his sister-in-law thinks. I can't figure out why he's talking about relatives. "Kathryn says that I won't be able to commit to a woman as long as my mother is alive," he says.

"I don't do anything halfway."

"I do everything halfway. You commit to things, I don't," Jack says.

"You're right. There's the heart versus the head."

"What do you mean by that?"

"My head tells me to let you go. That this will never work because you say that you don't love me, that you don't know what you want. But my heart hangs on." *I can't believe I have to spell this out.* I pause to find my words. "You're not emotionally . . ."

"Available?" Jack says, finishing my sentence.

"Perhaps. I was going to say 'open.'" *He has heard all of this before.* "What do you even want from me, Jack?"

"I could do with a friend. I need a friend."

"I am not going to be your buddy," I say, my voice cracking. "We both know the friends thing doesn't work."

As we finish packing up, Jack hovers and stays close. A reassuring hand on the small of my back. Carries my bags, talks to me softly. Like I'm ill. Like I'm some kind of goddamn mental patient. My feelings toward him ricochet between anger, resentment, love. And a pathetic gratitude for the smallest kindnesses.

On the ride to the airport, I close my eyes and lean my head on his shoulder and he wraps his big arm around me. The driver is telling Jack that when he's not driving a cab, he works as a comedian. *Comedian. Perfect. Because this is all such a fucking joke.* I remind myself to try to remember this. Because these will be some of my last moments with Jack.

We are both early for our flights, and we sit down together to share a sandwich. We both agree immediately on what it will be. A BLT with avocado. *Why can't the rest of this be this easy?*

I am less shaky. There are French fries and salty pickles and hot coffee.

We aren't talking and then we hear a song. "You only know you love her when you let her go . . ." and Jack begins singing along. He is singing and looking at me. I stare back. I am empty.

"And you let her go . . ."

I gaze out the window and watch the planes a little longer. "I should go to my gate," I say, slipping my credit card into the waitress's hand as she walks by.

Jack's flight is leaving from Terminal A and mine from B. We stand in the middle, at the intersection of both, and put our arms around each other and embrace.

"Let's talk. Can I call you?" Jack asks.

I say nothing. I don't know what to say, I cannot find any words. I'm numb.

"Can I call you?" Jack says again, this time more slowly, more loudly.

"I don't know."

"Okay, I'm going to call you," he says. "Text me and let me know that you got home safe."

I turn toward the security line and walk a few steps. Then I stop and turn around. Jack has stopped and is looking at me, too. And then we come back to each other. We touch forehead to forehead and press noses together. He kisses the tip of my nose. We embrace again. And then we let go.

♥

CHAPTER 21

Just Rip Off the Band-Aid

After Charleston, there are days of cooling off. Heavy silence and pain.

At first, I don't want contact. I am done. Need to just rip off the Band-Aid, cut my losses, move on. I've made an utter fool of myself, laid my cards on the table, and he simply doesn't want me.

I return to the dating books during my many moments of self-doubt. Zero contact now, they say. Give it breathing room and if he changes his mind, he'll be back. Don't be his buddy, pen pal, stop propping it up—let him feel your absence. That is the best and only hope. But after a few days, I weaken, reconsider. I text Jack:

> My primal sobbing the other night is shocking and embarrassing to me. I didn't know that was in there. I apologize for you having to witness it. Thank you for comforting me.
>
> The best I can come up with is that it's an indicator of the depth of my feelings for you. And my disappointment. That after nearly six months, it doesn't look like we want the same things.
>
> I'm also very anxious about seeing my father next week.

Jack replies:

> Don't be anxious about your visit to your father—it will be good.
>
> No problem on the emotion. I was happy to hold you through it.

And I tell him that I'm sorry. That it's all just hurt piled onto hurt. And then later in the week, we have some long conversations by phone, trying to sort through what I've been calling our "fundamental incompatibility." He disagrees that we're fundamentally incompatible and argues that I've broken up with him due to an "artificial deadline." I counter that it's not artificial, but that things have become too difficult to bear and I'd keep going if I could.

"I love hard, I love deeply. And I know you'll never be able to meet me there," I say. And he doesn't have a response. "When two people want the same things at the same time, it takes off like a house on fire." And he agrees.

Another big conversation comes Sunday. The day after I've run my third half-marathon. I'm exhausted but satisfied that I've completed another race—something unthinkable a year ago. I've been busy cooking all day because I've got a dozen friends coming for Sunday dinner. It's a housewarming party of sorts, celebrating this new life I've worked so hard to build. Food, warmth, love, friends around the table. In this conversation, Jack and I talk about his emotional distance. And he says, "But you're bored by the emotionally available men you're dating, so spend time with me." And he's practically mocking me that I always return to him and that I crave more from him. That he's the one I want. And then he adds, "I enjoy being with you, but I don't have to be with you." And those words hit me like a punch in the stomach. It's perhaps the final blow, the final straw.

"This isn't ever going to work, is it?" I say.

And Jack says, "I'm going to close by wishing you a good dinner party, visit with your father, and if you ever want to see me again, give me a call. And promise me that you're not going to be sad," and he hangs up.

♥

I am beyond emotionally exhausted. I have had it with Jack, dating, I have had it with men, full stop.

And Alton. That guy is getting on my last nerve. He continues to pester, so I've texted and let him know again, in no uncertain terms, that I'm only interested in his friendship, nothing else. And I've mentioned that the man in Boston and I are done. To which Alton has sent me an email:

> Dear Holly,
>
> It sounds like you have a new perspective on yourself and life, which will bring you much happiness.
>
> We all need to stop our engines in the water and reflect at times. The most difficult promises to keep are often those which we make with ourselves. I admire your honesty and conviction. I am proud to be your friend because you have raised the sails of your self-esteem and are headed on course in the right direction!
>
> I also believe that friendship and respect are the two most important cornerstones in any relationship. It really takes time to know someone before you can enjoy true sharing, real intimacy.

I'm sorry to hear of your past experiences—but remember, Holly, those are now behind you, provided you are true to yourself. You are too bright and beautiful a lady to ever allow these unworthy men to cloud your brilliant future.

Happy to be your platonic friend as you suggest. By the way, I saw something in a shop window over the weekend—just a little thing—that reminded me of you and if you have time I'd like to catch up—I've had some interesting developments in my life, too, to share with you. I am in New York and Connecticut tomorrow. Any chance we could meet up? I also have a small favor to ask of you.

Ever your friend,
Alton

Difficult promises to ourselves indeed.
A small favor?

♥

Date #50: Somehow Familiar

My heart is pretty broken.

I'm considering getting off all apps and taking a break from dating. I need time to heal. And here I am, only halfway through Joan Rivers's challenge. I had no idea this would be so wrenching.

Online, I read through some last emails. Someone named Miles has written:

> "I don't want to sound strange, or like a stalker, but I know that I've seen you before. It's been bothering me but I finally figured it out! Last weekend I saw you dancing with your daughter in the courtyard outside The Whelk in Westport. You looked happy and beautiful. You're very tall. I'd like to meet you."

I study Miles's picture and realize that he looks familiar to me, too. I'd noticed him from a distance—a good-looking, dark-haired man was sitting at a table outside with two other men. It had been a warm summer night, a band played in the courtyard, and Evie and I danced and laughed and ate ice cream. This coincidence felt like fate and helped me brush aside my broken heart for a little while and accept a date with him.

I meet Miles, a Buddhist former actor now financial advisor.

But I learn he's actually still married, is going through a difficult divorce, and is having a hard time adjusting to his new life. He is deeply unhappy. I politely finish my drink and excuse myself, saying I need to get home to my daughter.

♥

CHAPTER 22

Lost Children

Date #51: The Original Stranger

My Real Dad.

It's just lunch, I tell myself, trying to calm a swelling panic if I think about it too much. I want to retreat to a place of distant cool, like the woman I was when I wore a business suit and pearls and handled everything else but raw emotion.

I don't need you anymore.

He just happens to be the man who helped bring me into this world, but for whatever reason, exited my life. He was never involved, just a genetic contributor.

My friends ask if I'm okay and what I will say to him, and I've been shrugging and saying I'm going to wing it and then I change the subject. There's no plan. Maybe I'm in big-time denial, but if I overthink it, I'll probably chicken out. Like some playground pissing match, it was partly the fear of being labeled "chicken" that got me into this situation in the first place. *Jack.*

Because the past is done and my childhood is over. I'm a parent now and there are no do-overs here. I don't need parenting—I'm one myself.

If the double-dog-dare from Jack started all of this, it's my Aunt Sarah and Uncle Ray who made it reality. Sarah is my father's younger sister by six years, and Ray, her husband. Happily married childhood sweethearts, they are accustomed to taking care of people. Sarah is a retired nurse, and Ray, a former police detective. They've raised two kids and are grandparents now. I've seen Ray and Sarah only a few times in my life.

As the day approaches, Ray calls. It's interesting that it's Ray and not Sarah, since Sarah is the blood relative, but it's okay. Ray is warm and always ready with a joke. I imagine that when Ray was a cop, suspects just confessed simply because you want to please the man—he's such a likable guy.

So Ray reassures me and says the plan is that he and Sarah will be there when I step off the plane and then together we will drive two hours to have lunch with my father. After the meal, we will turn around and drive back. I will spend the night at their house in Toronto, and in the morning, they will return me to the airport and I'll fly home. Easy peasy.

Everything is set, and I keep expressing my thanks for their efforts to make this reunion possible. Then, a day or two before, Ray calls again. "A bit of a wrinkle," he says.

"Wrinkle?"

"Your dad plans on bringing his girlfriend."

"What?"

"He wants to bring Katy."

"Who is Katy?"

"Might be his girlfriend."

"Girlfriend? I thought he was married."

"Argh . . ." Ray laughs a little nervously. "Well, he still is married, but they're separated, and he's got this Katy—girlfriend or roommate, I'm not sure what they are to each other. They live together."

Heavy silence. "Who is she?"

"I don't know much about her, to be honest, Holly. She's younger and they live together. I think she helps take care of him."

"Like a paid caregiver or something?"

"No."

"Younger?"

"Forties, I think," Ray says

"Forties? My age."

"I guess that's right."

My mind somersaults in several directions. She's my age and he's bringing her to lunch with me, the daughter he abandoned as a baby? My father, who is almost eighty years old? "Ray—I mean—is he afraid to come by himself?"

"Don't know. It's what he said on the phone this morning."

A rush of hurt, but another part of me is urging to just calm down. So I say to Ray, "Look, I'm sure you understand this, but I've been waiting a lifetime for this moment. I just need some time alone with him. Doesn't he at least owe me that?"

"Yes," Ray says. "And Sarah and I will make sure that you get that time."

"How?"

"Maybe Katy comes for part of the lunch and then Sarah and I will excuse ourselves, taking her with us, so you get some time alone with your dad?"

I'm still incredulous. *She doesn't belong here*. Yet Ray has offered a reasonable compromise. "I guess that makes sense."

We hang up and I sit there at my desk, staring out the window, feeling like I just lost something again. Like I'd happened upon the smallest shard of something very dear, that I'd always wanted, but now it's lost again. *Why, Dad, is it always about a woman?*

♥

My Aunt Sarah is there once I clear Canadian Immigration, standing trim with her short, smartly cut hair streaked with gray, in her plaid blazer, shoulders back, perfect posture. She gives me a friendly hug. "Ray is waiting out in the car," she says, pulling out her cell phone. "I've got her," she says into it.

Ray is at the curb with the car running, and he, too, gives me a quick hug. Sarah jumps in up front, I'm in the back, like the little kid. *Like a time warp*. We pull away and begin driving north. I look out at the gray, overcast sky. I'm back in Canada. I'm the little kid in the back seat again, the kid plotting my escape to New York, to anywhere, anywhere but here. "When was the last time you've seen my father?" I ask, breaking the silence.

Sarah and Ray look at each other. "When was it?" Sarah says.

"Maybe three or four years ago?" Ray says. They have the intimate communication of a close, long-married couple.

"Yes, I think it was at his wedding, maybe," Sarah says.

That would be wedding Number Four.

"Oh." Their answer surprises me. They live reasonably close to each other, and then I realize that I don't really know much about their relationship with my dad.

"I've been doing some research on the family history," Ray says. "Genealogy has become a hobby."

"And we were going through some of your grandmother's things recently and we found an old newspaper clipping. An obituary."

"Obituary?"

"For my sister," Sarah says.

"What?"

"Shock to me, too," Sarah answers. "She was full term, but stillborn. Yet they named her and placed a death notice in the newspaper."

"Josephine," Ray says.

"Josephine." I let it sink in. "Grandma and Grandpa never told you?"

"Never," Sarah answers.

"Wow." I stare out the window, watching the passing countryside. Farms where the corn has been harvested, stalks bent and beginning to yellow in the fields. "They'd put the notice in the paper, so everyone else knew . . .?" I say, my mind drifting to my few memories of my father's parents, suddenly revising my understanding of them. Proud, hardworking, somewhat private people, with a close circle of friends.

"I've been wondering the same thing. What other secrets did they keep from us?"

"Stoic, that generation," Ray says.

"To carry that grief around for a lifetime and never speak of it," I say, remembering my grandmother. A tiny woman, barely over five feet tall, enormous blue eyes with a mind and tongue as sharp as a blade.

"I'd always wanted a sister," Sarah says, quietly.

"Does my father know about this?" I ask.

"We don't think so," Ray says. "We've been trying to find where the stillborn is buried."

The Stillborn. They call her The Stillborn. I don't know if I can handle all of this. What the hell is all of this, anyway? "Well, maybe we mention it another time. There's enough going on at this lunch already," I say and we all laugh.

Now we are silent for a stretch. I begin to think more carefully about what's about to happen and how I really feel about my father. I marvel, as I have so many times before, about how he abandoned not one but three families. Amelia, his first wife, and their two children, Heather and Aaron, my half-brother and sister were the first casualties. And even after Amelia died of cancer following their divorce, my father never claimed his children. Heather and Aaron were split up between relatives—Heather raised by an aunt while Aaron was raised by a distant relative.

Next was my mother and me, whom he left when Mom was seven months pregnant with Margot and I was still in diapers. He was having an affair with Jess, a woman he worked with. He divorced my mother and married Jess, officially adopting her toddler son, Milan. Jess and Milan were eventually abandoned, too.

"I've got some old photographs, too, that I want to show you," Sarah says.

"I'd like that," I say.

"Photos from the time when your father ran away," she says.

"Ran away?"

"Haven't you heard that story?" Sarah says, with a nervous laugh. "When I was nine and your father was fifteen, he just disappeared?"

"I'm not sure . . ."

"We didn't know. He ran away. Grandma and Grandpa were beside themselves, and I was so worried about what had happened to my big brother. Every day I'd come home from school, hoping that he'd be back."

"That is awful," I say, but that hope is all too familiar. *Coming home from school, hoping for a miracle. That one day he'd appear to save me.*

"And these are the days before the Internet where there's not the mass communications to find missing children," Sarah continues. "No missing kids on milk cartons yet. Grandma and Grandpa kept contacting the local police, hoping they'd find him. He was gone nine months. We didn't know if he was dead or alive. Finally, he was found."

"Where?" I ask.

"Living way in the Northwest Territories. He'd lied about his age and he'd found a job and was living up there," Sarah says.

"Northwest Territories? Why there?" I say.

"No one ever figured that out," Ray says. "But your grandparents scraped together what little money they had to try to help him."

"They sent him to a military boarding school," Sarah adds. "Boarding school helped sort him out for awhile."

My father has been running his whole life.

And Ray, Sarah, and I continue to talk, and I realize that this visit with my father today is not only difficult for me, but it's wrenching for Sarah, too. My father, her big brother, has brought her pain and abandonment, too. This is why she hasn't seen him in years.

♥

We've arrived at the small, lakeside town where my father lives. A place with less than twenty thousand in off season but then swells when the summertime population invades from Toronto. There's a quaint main street lined with brick buildings. A post office, a few banks and churches, a library, a handful of tourist shops.

To my surprise, my father has chosen a Greek restaurant for lunch. For some reason, this strikes me as funny as I realize I was expecting some generic joint with Canadian-American food, but instead, cue the folk dancers and ouzo for comic relief. I will later learn that my father once lived in Sardinia and that the food at this restaurant reminds him of that time. There is so much that I don't know about this man.

Sarah, Ray, and I arrive just minutes before my father. We are seated at a long, rustic wooden table. The restaurant is bustling with locals. I am starting to feel a sense of unreality about all of this, not fully believing it is happening.

From my seat, I see a tall figure at the door.

My father arrives hunched over a walker yet he's somehow still statuesque, still striking, looking younger than his nearly eighty years. I watch him slowly make his way toward me, watery blue eyes locked with mine, a broken smile across his weathered face.

I stand and take a few steps forward to embrace him. "You got tall," he says. Everything has grown quiet. And over his shoulder, smiling shyly, is Katy. There's something childlike about her, something unusual. No makeup, dull, coarsely cut, brown hair, clothes that are too small for her ample body. "This is Katy," my father says.

"Hi," I say, pulling away from my father and awkwardly shaking her hand. She smiles shyly.

"It's good to meet, finally," Katy says.

Finally. Am I going to survive this?

My father and I sit down across from one another, Katy to my immediate left, Ray at the table's head and Sarah at the opposite end. We are handed custom menus for the meal, and I realize that my father has made special arrangements.

The owner of the restaurant comes over to take our drink orders and my father says to her, "This is my daughter." The owner makes a fuss over me and my father beams.

My father has selected the main course: rabbit. This again strikes me as comical, unexpected, especially since I don't eat rabbit or duck, having had both as childhood pets, but how would he know? I will choke down the rabbit, along with the rest of the meal, which actually turns out to be otherwise excellent. The restaurant owner says that the cook came in early this morning to cook this special meal, to marinate the rabbit. That this dish is only made for holidays and special celebrations and I am moved by that.

The group conversation begins with the usual pleasantries—the weather, how was my flight, and then Evie. I pull a few old photographs from my wallet of Evie and they're passed around the table. The wide-eyed baby; the coy, sunhat-wearing toddler; the three-year-old flying a kite with her father on Good Friday, a Bermuda tradition.

I learn that, around my age, my father suffered a stroke, and ever since, his speech is somewhat slurred and halting. I find I must listen very carefully to understand what he's saying. After a time, I adapt to the rhythm and intonation of his speech, and once

I do, I discover he's got a marvelous sense of humor. That at least half of what he says is a joke, or teasing.

The group around the table has begun to relax. Jokes are being cracked and then it hits me—we all share the same sense of humor. Is it in the genes? For a fleeting moment, it feels like family that has been together forever.

After dessert, Ray and Sarah whisk Katy away even though she's protested and wanted to linger over tea.

Dad and I are finally alone. He grasps my hands across the table. He is trembling. We meet each other's eyes, knowing there isn't much time. Not today, or in the future. I look into the eyes that are my eyes, the face that is my face and the face of my sister, Margot. "I wouldn't have recognized you on the street," he says, and I nod, feeling overwhelmed by the raw accuracy of the fact. We have always been strangers. He's silent for a moment, studying me. "You're beautiful," he says, gently.

I stare down at the marred wooden tabletop, the nicks and scratches blurring before my eyes, and tell myself not to cry. So many years of buried pain and an anguish that I didn't even know was there feels like it's beginning to break me open. I am here with my father—my real father. I take a deep breath and recall Jack saying those same words to me just a few weeks ago: "You're beautiful."

I struggle to meet Dad's gaze again. "I love you," he says.

"I love you, too," I say in return, so easily, so simply, it's just true, and with those words, an inexplicable peace washes through me. Now Dad and I are both openly crying. I don't even try to hold back anymore, this is all so out of my control, and haven't I been trying to control so much for so long? I see my father's lined but still handsome, tear-stained face, the wide, clear eyes, and it suddenly hits me: the similarities to another older, handsome man's face. Jack helped bring me here. He's at this table, too. The lovable rogue, the heartbreaker whom I love, helped bring me to the biggest heartbreaker of my life: my father.

It won't come right away; many more months will pass before I begin to understand what this moment has given me. Healing, yes, but a knowledge, at my deepest core, that I am beautiful, inside and out. In spite of my imperfections, the nicks and the scrapes, or the warts and idiosyncrasies, as Jack would say. That I'm worthy of love.

♥

I've returned from the ladies' room. I needed a moment to pull myself together, and I'm guessing he did, too. There is a little time left before the others will return, and Dad I now speak of other things besides us.

He asks me about Evie, and he grins as he hands me a teddy bear that he has bought for her. I tell him that she talked early and hasn't stopped since, that she's smart and funny and plays the violin. That she's the best thing ever.

Dad tells me that a few years back, he and my mother reestablished contact. I don't say too much and just listen. He squeezes my hand and says, "I told her that our girl really knows how to handle a car," he says. I'm baffled by the compliment because when has he ever seen me drive? Has he confused me with another of his lost children? And what's interesting is that how I drive is something that my stepfather criticized me for and, more recently, David. Just who might have I become if my father had been in my life?

"You've done well. You have more than one house?" Dad asks.

I nod.

"Good for you."

Please don't think this was easy. Please don't think that you not being there didn't matter.

"Your sister is having a hard time. Why not you?"

"We're different people. I'm a lot tougher than Margot? I don't know," I say. How can I answer a question like that?

Dad nods. "I'm trying to help her out where I can."

"That's good of you," I say. Dad has almost nothing and yet he's sending money to Margot now? I didn't know.

Later, I will say good bye to my father and we will talk of another visit, sometime in the future, when I will bring Evie, too.

♥

Back in the car on the drive back to Toronto with Ray and Sarah, my phone rings. "Hello?"

"Did you forgive him?" a little voice says. I catch my breath. It's Evie. *Did you forgive?*

"Yes, sweetie, I did." Not once have I explained this visit in those terms.

Evie asks about Ray and Sarah and says she wants to speak with Sarah. I hand the phone over. "Has your mother bought you a pony yet?" Sarah says. Ray and I crack up.

♥

"Do you miss police work?" I ask Ray as he cuts into his steak, back in Toronto. We've all agreed today has been a success.

"Sometimes," Ray says.

"You must have seen some difficult things in your career?" Ray and Sarah exchange a look.

"In the beginning, it was hard on our marriage," Sarah says. "He would shut down and I didn't know how to reach him."

"Nothing prepares you," Ray says. "When I was in my early twenties, just starting out, I was posted way up in northern Ontario, working for the Ontario Provincial Police. Back in those days, you didn't have a partner, so it was just me and I literally had a couple hundred kilometers to patrol by myself. One night, very late, in the middle of the winter, there was a call of trouble out at the Indian reservation. That a little boy, a six-year-old, was missing. I arrive and no one wants to tell me anything. No one will talk, everyone back in those days was afraid of the police. Then finally someone tells me that they think the little boy is in the lake and I wade in to the black water. He's floating face down and his body is ice cold." Ray pauses and looks away for a second. "I pull him out, try to get him to breathe . . ." Ray's voice is cracking. "I try a long time, but he's just gone. I call out for the parents. 'Where is this boy's mother?' 'Where is this boy's father?' I'm yelling but no one will say anything. No one will claim him. And there's no ambulance to call and the nearest hospital and coroner is more than an hour away. So I wrap his body in a wool blanket and lay him in the back of the cruiser and we drive."

♥

After dinner, Sarah will show me the family photos. There's a class photograph, an old black and white. "Can you pick out your dad?" she asks. I cannot. He's the only boy wearing a tie; it hangs well below his belt. I'm guessing he borrowed it from my grandfather.

Then there's another black and white, this one of my grandparents' farmhouse where Sarah and my father were raised in northern Ontario. It looks like summertime, everything lush and lit by sunshine. My grandparents were gifted gardeners. "Here is where your dad slid down the roof and disappeared," she says, pointing to a bedroom window. He slid down the roof in the wintertime, landed in the snow, and ran away.

Dad ran away. I ran away, too.

Later, in bed, in Sarah and Ray's downstairs guestroom that smells musty and like my grandparents' house, I struggle to fall asleep. Too many images in my head, too many swirling emotions. I cannot stop thinking of the stillborn Aunt Josephine and the drowned little boy in the icy lake whose parents would not claim him. And my father, the runaway boy who grows up to become the runaway man, and Sarah, the nine-year-old, wondering if her big brother whom she loves so much is dead or alive. I think of myself, too, the young girl always longing for her real father, wondering if he would ever claim me. He did today. *This is my daughter. You're beautiful. I love you.*

♥

Sarah gets up early to make me breakfast: homemade muffins, fruit salad, and yogurt. Still in her housecoat (as they call bathrobes in Canada), she watches me eat as she nurses a large mug of coffee and cuddles Francesca, her King Charles Spaniel. Ray drives me to the airport.

On the flight home to New York, I am someone I don't know. There is something wrong with me. Maybe it's the buried grief leading up to this reunion, the denied dread and hopeful anticipation, the reality, and now just trying to make sense of it all. It has hit me with shocking force. I sit in a window seat on the plane, grateful to have only empty seats around me. I curl into the window, shield my face with a hand, and silently weep. The tears just keep coming and coming, and the longer they fall, the more I fear they may never stop. Something in me has burst. Then I feel something. The flight attendant squeezes my shoulder and jams a wad of tissues into my hand and silently walks away. This makes me cry harder.

♥

As the plane is landing in New York, I check my phone. There is a text from Jack:

> "Good luck with the old coot this weekend J."

Old coot? No.

I know. He's just trying to lighten things up. Jack and I haven't communicated in days.

I text him my thanks. That the visit has already taken place and I'm almost home now.

He apologizes for confusing the date and asks how it went.

"One of the hardest days of my life," is my answer. Radio silence after that. Jack does not reply.

♥

CHAPTER 23

A Small Favor

Date #52: Reliable to a Fault

Alton's favor: he needs a date to a black-tie event, and he's wondering if I might accompany him, as a friend. The dinner is for charity, a good cause. I figure I need to stay busy, distract myself from fixating on Jack and the upheaval of seeing my father, so I agree. Then Alton discloses that the event is in Newport, Rhode Island. Rhode Island, which, depending upon the onerous traffic on the I-95, can mean three to four hours driving, each direction, from my house.

"Rhode Island?"

"You can stay overnight on my yacht. You'll have your own state room and my staff will take the very best care of you. I'll be at my house."

A few days earlier, when I was in Canada visiting my father, Alton sent an email saying he could send a plane to pick me up in Canada and deliver me to Rhode Island and also suggested that I wear flats or low heels to the event. That lower heels might be more "comfortable" for dancing. I told him I would make my own travel arrangements, thank you very much, and I began to suspect that his suggestion has less to do with my comfort and more to do with my height. I'm already regretting agreeing to accompany him, but I'm a bit of a time traveler, too. My word is my bond. If I say I'm going to do something, I damn well do it.

I pack a black dress and medium-high heels. Screw flats. No man is going to tell me how to dress.

When I arrive at the marina, Alton Manley is standing at the entrance, dressed in Bermuda shorts, waving. I stop the car and he jumps in. "Lovely to see you," he says, kissing both of my cheeks. "This way," he says, in his accent, directing me where to park. *He's sounding more British today.*

There are enormous yachts everywhere. "This one over there," Alton says, "arrived last night. It belongs to Oprah."

"Wow," I say, noting the yacht's sleek design and jaunty, little red helicopter on the upper deck, making ship-to-shore excursions that much easier. "I love the helicopter!"

Alton sniffs. "Her vessel is rather flimsy. It cannot cross the Atlantic," he says. But Alton Manley's *All Man* can. "That's what happens when you come into money but don't understand what you're buying," Alton adds.

The *All Man* indeed seems a solid vessel, built in the 1960s, meticulously maintained, updated and refurbished, a bit of a battleship, not that I know much about anything that floats. I did take sailing lessons once and hated being stuck for hours out on Long Island Sound with no wind, no bathroom, getting soaked by a cold rain. I do know enough, at least, to remove my shoes prior to boarding.

Once aboard, I'm introduced to the woman whom, I later will understand, wears many hats, from personal chef, steward, purser, boat wrangler, to chambermaid. She is a one-woman show. She *is* "The Staff."

"May I use the ladies' room?" I ask Alton, knowing full well that on boats it's called the "head," but there's no way I'm saying *that* word, aloud. Not giving this guy any ideas.

During my brief respite, I check my phone. Rose has texted me photos from *Gilligan's Island*, including headshots of Ginger and Mr. Howell. Alton is indeed Thurston, with a touch of Austin Powers. I want to get back in my car and drive home and sleep for three days. I'm just not up for this, but I've made it this far. I dry my hands on the restroom towel and note they are monogrammed with *All Man*.

I step out and Alton is standing right there by a built-in mahogany desk covered with framed photographs. Photos of him hunting with Prince Charles, or another, at a London charity event that he seems to have organized with Joan Collins, or, wait—is that Elton John? "I thought we might go out on the boat before dinner," Alton says.

"In that case, let me get a sweater."

"I suggest, then, that you open your gifts."

"Gifts?" Now I'm really uncomfortable.

"Come, sit here," he says, leading me to a wood-paneled sitting room with heavy furniture and velvet drapery. I sit and wait.

Alton reappears with three beautifully wrapped boxes, in shimmery white paper with bright blue bows. "Really . . .?" I say.

"They are modest," Alton reassures.

I open the largest first, and inside is a canvas carry-all customized with the logo for *All Man*. "Oh! Thank you."

The second contains two baseball caps, emblazoned with, you guessed it—*All Man*. "I thought you might give one to Evie," he says.

"Ohh . . . thank you."

And last, but not least, a blue polar fleece embroidered with . . . *All Man*. "My goodness. Very thoughtful."

"You can wear that jumper now," Alton says. "It gets chilly." I slip it over my head. "Let's be off," he says.

The Staff is a woman of many talents and she helps Alton bring his smaller craft, a wood hulled motor boat, alongside *All Man* so that I might easily board without falling in the drink. As we speed away, I stare off at Oprah's yacht, deciding that if Alton pulls any funny business, I'm staying with her. Oprah would save me.

♥

Newport, Rhode Island, is a seaside city known not only for its yachts, but also its grand history, mansions, and wealth. Once a major port city, it has beautifully preserved colonial buildings and you feel as though you are back in time.

Alton's tour follows the rugged coast, getting close enough so that I might see the mansions in detail. He points out who lives where, which party he attended in which house, who slept with whom, what the scandals are. I listen and comment politely.

The sun begins to drop and we are bathed in a warm, amber light. It's a beautiful evening, though windy, and I'm struck by what a romantic moment this should be. If only. If only I had feelings for this man, and what's worse is he's trying so hard. My mind drifts to when Jack took me out on his boat in Boston.

Alton glances at his watch, a massive Swiss timepiece that's probably worth more than my car. "Shall we go in? It's time to dress for dinner."

Back on board *All Man*, Alton leads me to my state room. "Each room has a theme," he says. "Yours is America!"

"So that explains this," I say, picking up a red, white, and blue throw pillow off one of the twin beds. Alton grins proudly.

Next, Alton spends a long time explaining every knob, dial, latch, door, function, and feature of my state room, as though I'm never going to figure out how to work a shower or an air conditioner simply because it's on a boat. "Anything you need," he adds, "anything at all—I'm just down the hall."

Down the hall? Alton isn't staying at his house. He's staying here.

I thank him, he leaves, and I lock the door. I locate a chest of drawers to put away some of my things and notice a sign:

> Guests are kindly asked to keep their rooms tidy at all times, with luggage, etcetera, put away in closets in the event of *All Man* tours.

Your cooperation is greatly appreciated.

Tours?

In my bathroom are more monogrammed towels as well as *All Man* soap, in a scent of English roses.

I dress, and when I appear, Alton lavishes praise for my dress and choice of diamond earrings. I see him glance disapprovingly at my shoes, but he says nothing. In a funny twist of coincidence, Alton inquires as to the designer of my dress, and she turns out to be the sister of the man he challenged to the duel in the Caribbean.

Prior to dinner, there's a mini photo shoot. The Staff has been instructed to photograph us before the big event. I humor Alton by scrunching down, trying to appear shorter. He will later email me some of the photos, saying what a lovely couple we make.

The dinner, held at a waterside location in an enormous tent, is tedious. We are seated at a table of strangers who barely speak to us. The food is meh. There are multiple speeches, lasting about an hour in total. We clap politely after each. I can play this game, having done it many times before back in my Wall Street days and then in the role of corporate wife. This is work. But then, finally, it's time for the dancing. "Would you like to dance?" Alton asks.

On the dance floor, I feel stiff and uninspired. I force a smile and focus on letting him lead, trying to anticipate his next move, backward, in my medium heels.

My mind keeps slipping back to Canada and my father. I am still just so very sad. I can't stop thinking of everything that's happened, how to make sense of it all. And Jack. I can't stop thinking about him, either.

♥

Back aboard the *All Man* in the wood-paneled sitting room with the heavy drapes and the brass, nautical accents, Alton suggests a nightcap. "Would you like some wine?" he asks holding up a bottle.

"What . . .?" I pause. "Oh my goodness!"

"Yes, I remembered you mentioned this is your favorite," Alton says. He's bought six bottles of it.

This is what men do when they really care. They pay attention.

Alton pours us each a glass of the wine. "Tell me about your visit with your father. And what's happened with this man from Boston . . ."

We sit. I barely touch the wine, and I spend a good part of the conversation crying. Will I ever be able to talk about any of this without crying? Alton tries to take my hand to comfort me. "I'm sorry. I can't," I say, pulling back my hand. "I can only be your friend. It's unfair for you to think otherwise."

"I understand," Alton says and he listens patiently. "I hope in the future he understands what a gem you are. That he treats you better," he says.

"Thank you. You've been very kind. I really should go to bed."

Alton walks me to my room, gives me a hug, and wishes me a good night's sleep.

♥

Date #53: Rum is the Secret

The next morning, I awake around 8:30 and dress. I've slept surprisingly well and there's been no sound or sign of Alton. Quietly, I climb the stairs to the main deck before I'm pounced on by The Staff. "Alton has instructed that I make you banana pancakes," she says.

"Oh." Mandatory banana pancake eating aboard the *All Man*? Okay.

The Staff directs me outside where the table has been set for my breakfast. My seat has a great view of the shimmering ocean, the blue sky dotted with fluffy, white clouds, and Oprah's yacht. I can still swim for it if things get ugly.

"Where is Alton?" I ask.

"He's at church," The Staff replies. "How do you take your coffee?"

While The Staff prepares my coffee, I smooth a cloth napkin across my lap. Monogrammed *All Man*. There's a centerpiece of fresh flowers and the sound of flags snapping in the breeze. This isn't a terrible way to wake up on a Sunday morning.

As I'm halfway through the mandatory pancakes topped with maple syrup, butter, and a side of bacon, Alton arrives. "Good morning!" he declares, kissing my cheek and handing me a bouquet of yellow roses.

"Thank you," I say, taking the flowers and inwardly recoiling. *Note to self for hundredth time: friendship arrangement not working.* Alton immediately calls for The Staff to handle my roses.

"How was church?" I ask.

"It was a very nice service. I actually belong to three churches, depending upon my location. One at home, one here in Newport, and one in London . . ."

"I see."

"Did you sleep well?" Alton asks.

"Very much so, thanks."

"How do you like the pancakes?"

"Delicious!" They really are.

"Rum is the secret ingredient." Rum, he tells me, from the Caribbean island where he'd challenged that man to a duel. *All roads lead back to the duel.* "So are you up for a walk this morning? I thought we might take a stroll."

"That's very kind, but I need to get going shortly," I say.

"You have something planned?"

"Uh, yes." *Getting the hell out of here.* I feel my mouth twist. *Is it obvious how miserable I am?*

"Well, a short walk, then."

"Sounds good."

Alton leads me down the dock toward a walkway that hugs the harbor. He grabs my hand. I walk a few steps holding his hand, pondering the most polite way to get it back to its rightful owner without making this completely awkward at the end of this crazy weekend. Even keel, pun intended. I drop to my knee to tie my shoelace. Now I stroll, hands in pockets, which works well, as Alton chatters away with witty facts about Newport. Not too far away, we see a man in a kilt, practicing his bagpipes. For some reason, the Scotsman makes the entire experience that much more comical. I'd hide under that kilt if it meant escaping Alton.

Finally, it is time to leave. Alton walks me to my car, carrying my bag. Without warning, he lets himself into my car and sits in the passenger seat. "Here, let me adjust your GPS," he says. "I think this will work better."

Not arguing. Anything to get out of here faster.

And of course, as luck would have it, after his adjustments, I become lost on the way home and end up driving an additional hour and a half out of my way. Coincidence? Perhaps. At any rate, I'm sure he meant well.

♥

CHAPTER 24

Fear and Intuition

Date #54: Dinner in Cambridge

A week ago, I finally broke down and just called Jack, heart pounding, hoping my voice wouldn't shake. Asked if he remembered that I'm going to be in Boston this weekend. "Do you still want to have dinner with Immie and Zara?" Immie and Zara are my friends visiting from England.

"I was hoping I'm still invited," Jack says. *Hoping?* He's made us reservations at a restaurant that he thinks Immie and Zara would like, a trendy place that should appeal since they're both young and hip, barely thirty years old.

Evie and our babysitter, who have come along, too, meet Immie and Zara for lunch and we all spend the afternoon together. I'd first met Immie eight years earlier at a writing course in the countryside of Cambridge, England. At the time, she was a PhD candidate at Oxford, writing her dissertation on Proust. In the years since, Immie has realized she's gay and has left academia to become a psychotherapist.

Zara is Immie's new love interest, whom I've never met before. Zara, too, is brilliant, with multiple degrees in mathematics from both Oxford and Cambridge. As we stroll through an art gallery that afternoon, they tell me they're thinking of getting married and starting a family and I enthusiastically agree. They seem wonderful together, at ease in each other's presence, the way they look at each other, always connected, whether it be through touch, glance, private joke.

Late afternoon, we go our separate ways until dinner time. Evie and the babysitter settle in for a night back at the hotel with movies and room service. Jack texts: "Can I pick you up?"

"Thank you."

I wait outside the hotel. It's late September, and the day has been unseasonably hot, in the eighties, a last blast of summer. How will it be seeing each other? We've been through so much these past few weeks.

My back is turned when he comes up behind me and touches my shoulder and

I startle. "Sorry I'm late," he says. He gives me a peck on the cheek and I follow him to his car.

"Are you ready to spend an evening with young British lesbians?" I say.

He laughs. "I am indeed."

Traffic is heavy on the drive to Cambridge; it takes us a good twenty-five minutes by the time we park the car. But the time together has helped us break the ice again; we've kept the conversation light.

The restaurant that Jack has selected is perfect. Craigie On Main is slightly bohemian with innovative food and a rock star chef. Jack pulls out the stops and orders a bottle of wine from the year of Immie and Zara's birth: 1986.

And Jack is absolutely charming and gentlemanly. Anytime one of us three women leaves the table for the ladies' room, he stands, which makes the three of us laugh and we push him back down in his seat. Conversation flows, and we spend most of the meal laughing.

After dinner, Jack and I say our goodbyes to Immie and Zara and walk to his car. "Do you want to get a drink?" Jack says.

"Okay . . ."

"There's some good bars around here. Or we could go back to my place and sit out on the deck. It's a nice night."

"Your place."

And the night is beautifully warm, much like a month ago when we were skinnydipping in the pool. We sit out on deck in the dark, sipping wine, staring out at the lights on the harbor, talking, talking. Sometimes we stop and kiss and hold each other. Sometimes we do a little more than that. Sometimes we laugh. It's all very natural, even as we talk about not being together anymore.

"I remember the first time you picked me up and carried me to the bed," I say. He squeezes my hand, and we are silent again for a while.

"I'm fucked up," he says. And he tells me that he didn't like my ultimatum and how that explains the "I enjoy being with you but don't need to be with you."

We talk a little about Nadia. I've wondered if they've reconciled, but his story is the same as before. "Some texting. Coffee every three or four months," he says.

He asks me about the visit with my father. I talk a long time with Jack about that and he listens patiently. "I'm sorry I never replied when you said meeting him was one of the toughest days of your life," Jack says.

"It's okay." *He remembers.*

"I didn't know what to say," Jack says.

And then it's back to us again. "Do you even know what I want?" I ask.

"Lasting love, a true partner, passion. A best friend."

His words stun. "Yes," I say. "Yes, that is exactly right." He understands perfectly. Maybe he's understood perfectly all along.

We talk more until the early hours of the morning. One of the last things he says to me is, "No matter what, you're really fucking hot."

I look at him, half amused, half exasperated. "Well, we've resolved fuck all," I answer.

Jack watches me fasten the strap on my high-heeled sandal. "Can you walk in those?" I shake my head. "Let me drive you," he says.

At the hotel, he gets out of the car, comes around and opens my door. We wrap our arms around one another, and it's still the most exquisite feeling in the world. This is where I long to be. I don't want to let go. And then he gives me one last, beautiful kiss.

Spinning through the hotel's revolving door, I shiver. An intuition and a fear that this was the last time I will ever see Jack Carver.

♥

The next morning on the way to Boston's New England Aquarium with Evie, I see a text has come in the night before from Alton:

> Hope all is well—just enjoying a wonderful evening at the Dorchester in London with Simon Cowell and Joan Collins. We are raising money for a children's hospice. Wish you were here with me.

He includes a glitzy shot of the hotel ballroom.

I reply that I'm in Boston. I say nothing about why I'm here, who I'm with, or any of it, and then Alton melts down. Perhaps it's simply the mention of Boston and he assumes I'm here because of Jack.

Alton texts that I ought not to remain in Jack's emotional debt simply because he encouraged me to see my father. "Hope you will be truly happy together and he treats you better. Bye."

Bye? Really?

But I owe him no explanation. I'm just so tired of Alton, Jack, all of this. I put my phone away in my handbag. Evie strolls happily at my side, enjoying the breeze off the water and the sunshine on her face. I love her little freckles, her smile, her joy. This is what I need to focus on. My beautiful little girl.

♥

Alton refuses to go quietly. "Your heart saw clearly when I gave you my card and you emailed me," he texts. "We have met for a reason."

So you can irritate me?

"Your recent texts have made me very uncomfortable," I reply. "Even my closest family and friends wouldn't offer unsolicited advice on what I should think and feel."

"My apologies," Alton writes. "I very much appreciate our friendship. I was only trying to help you navigate through some difficult emotional straits because I truly care for you. I want you to be happy, even if I'm not the lucky guy, because your happiness means more to me than my own. I thought we had touched each other's hearts."

I'm hurting you, Jack is hurting me. God only knows what, if anything, is hurting Jack. And so it goes.

♥

Date #55: Old Lesson Relearned

A lunch date with Vic, my new "neighbor," as he refers to himself. I show up to prove that I'm sincere about friendship, and I insist on picking up the check. I find myself wanting to be kind to Vic because he's a genuinely good man and I guess I feel guilty about disappointing him.

But walking back home after lunch, I question my sincerity. Did I enjoy myself? No. Should I spend time with a man I'm not interested in, even as a friend? Nope. Do I need to take responsibility for his hurt feelings? Yet again, no. Holly, you know better. My first responsibility is to me, not someone I barely know.

♥

It's early October, and I'm still miserable and pining for Jack and Alton still hasn't given up. He sends an email, dispatched from London, with the subject line "Connecticut and California Invitations," asking if I might know why his texts messages are being returned and would I be his date at a ball in Monterey, California. Additionally, this very week he plans on hosting a party on his yacht, coincidentally now moored just five minutes from my house. *Fool me once* . . . to which I reply:

Dear Alton,

I received your text and voice mail messages. Thank you.

As I indicated recently, your text messages sent while I was in Boston have made me very uncomfortable. I do not wish to continue a friendship or otherwise and ask that you no longer contact me.

I'm glad to have met you and appreciate your many kindnesses. I wish you all the best in finding your special someone.

Holly

London

Dear Holly,

Because you are such a warm and sensitive person, I understand how difficult it must have been for you to send me this message.

If your conscience feels better by using an email as an excuse to dismiss our friendship, then I hope you've found the consolation you need. I guess our friendship really didn't mean that much to you because you never gave me the chance to apologize or speak with you about it. But I do hope that I filled the void when Jack was less available to you.

I hope all is well with your dad and that he does meet Evie someday soon. You have been through some really challenging times when we all need a friend. I enjoyed our time together and was glad to be there for you when you needed me.

Remember that I shall always be your friend and be there for whenever you need me.

Fondly,

Alton

Alton B. Manley, CEO

Whiffley Capital

Oh, Alton.

♥

CHAPTER 25

Second Guesses

It's been a couple of weeks since Boston, and I still can't forget Jack. He's always there—a gnawing, empty ache. While I remind myself that I did the best I could these past six months, I still second-guess myself.

Did I put too much pressure on him? On us? Was I too impatient? Did the damn dating books that implore you not to waste time, to smoke out a man's true intentions, have too much of an influence?

Was I too raw and on edge and sensitive to rejection around the upheaval of meeting my father?

I decide to write Jack a letter, and before I can change my mind, stupidly, I mail it.

I tell Jack that I miss him, our daily communications, conversations, funny texts, our private jokes. How when I travel, he is the last person I text when the plane door closes and the first when I land. I tell him he's a charmer, he's my friend.

I say that I've been replaying the things we spoke of on his deck in Boston that last night and what a wonderful evening it was, in so many ways. How touching his efforts were to connect with my friends, his generosity. That I'll never forget the moment, on the drive home, when he took my hand and kissed it. That feeling of my hand in his.

And I admit that I wonder if I—if we—could have been more measured and found a middle ground? Did I simply panic when he said he didn't need me? When he didn't know if he wanted a relationship? Perhaps I did. It cut deeply.

I care deeply for him and I want him to be happy. I don't know if this is where our story ends, but I do know I'm so glad we've met.

♥

Date #56: The Socialist of Uruguay

Ignacio is one of my last online dates.

His photo is striking. Thick, stick-straight black hair, mysterious, deep eyes. Originally from Montevideo. "Montevideo!" I say, in our email exchange. "I've never met someone from there before."

"Read up on it," Ignacio writes, "before we meet."

A little bossy, but I do. In my mind, Montevideo is somewhere in South America, but no clue where. Just the word conjures up mystery. Google tells me that it's the capital of Uruguay, a small, coastal country in eastern South America, nestled between Argentina and Brazil.

We meet for lunch on a sunny, mid-week afternoon in Connecticut.

He arrives fifteen minutes late, and as he approaches the table, I'm not sure what to make of him. He's not unattractive and is in decent shape, which is obvious through his form-fitting lilac-colored dress shirt and neatly tailored pinstripe pants.

Ignacio is a lawyer. He's also someone who's lied about his status; he's still married, and he throws out this fact unapologetically. He tells me that his wife is crazy, is taking all of his money, and has turned the kids against him. An original script. Eventually he tires of complaining. "Are you a Republican?" he asks. "Because if you are, I think that would be a problem for me."

"Oh, are we talking politics already?"

"I am a socialist," he says boldly.

"Oh! I haven't met one of those since I left Canada." Now I'm picturing Ignacio in fatigues running through the jungles of Uruguay trying to stage a coup.

"I am an atheist," Ignacio says next.

"I'm agnostic," I answer. He blinks back at me for a few seconds. "You know . . . I allow for the possibility for the existence of God . . .?"

"I know what it means," he says. "Do you like dogs?"

"I do!" I say. *Finally, something we can agree on!*

"I do not like how they smell."

"Oh."

I glance at my watch. "Look at the time. I have to pick up my daughter." I ask the waiter for the check.

"Oh, I'm so glad you paid!" Ignacio exclaims as I hand over my credit card.

"What . . .?"

"I mean—what if I never see you again?" Ignacio says.

Count on it, dude.

"Let me walk you to your car," Ignacio says.

"It's okay, I'm not far—just up the street," I say.

"Oh, no, I insist," Ignacio says.

As we walk to the car, he grabs my arm. "Stop!" he says.

"What?"

He turns and points at our reflection in a store window. "Look!"

"What?"

"Are you taller than me?" he says, squinting. "Maybe by just an inch," he says.

I turn and continue striding up the street. "I really need to get going," and Ignacio hurries to catch up, eventually falling back in step.

"Wait!" Ignacio says, stopping me again. He points into another store window, moving closer in to measure more precisely. "No . . . I think we are the same size," he says.

Suddenly I'm an Olympic walker with a case of the trots. I cannot walk fast enough. "Gotta go!" I call over my shoulder.

"Wait!" Ignacio says. I've made it to my car.

"Nice meeting you," I say, half-heartedly, offering my hand.

"No kiss?" Ignacio says.

"No. Thank you." I jump in my car and hit the gas.

♥

Date #57: Brace Yourself

Emmet lives in Connecticut, is well traveled, German American, a lawyer, speaks French.

> **Emmet**: I hope you are well. We are all set for 8:30 p.m. for dinner.
>
> **Me**: Fantastic. Looking forward to meeting you.
>
> **Emmet**: Et moi aussi. But don't get your hopes up. Brace yourself for a disappointment. But a few glasses of wine should fix that.

I'm standing at the back by the bar when Emmet comes in. My first impression is pleasant surprise. He's tall and lean with sharp, chiseled features. Late fifties, early sixties, maybe. Around Jack's age. Why does everything always return to Jack?

Emmet has three grown sons and an ex-wife who lives in town. Everyone gets along.

Emmett asks me a lot of questions, rapid fire, frequently brushing my arm. He's been everywhere, from New Zealand and all over Asia to train treks through Russia. The man loves adventure, and he tells a good story.

As I walk home after dinner, I realize it felt good to have company tonight. If Emmet asks me out again, I'd go. It's good to be distracted from my tortured thoughts of Jack.

♥

Date #58: She's Not the Only One Who Suffered

Not an online date. This is a set up. This is the elusive television executive Al, who was too busy for me back in the summer but has resurfaced, setting a date and a time and has actually shown up, in the flesh, to take me out for a very nice dinner.

My real estate agent—the one who says she's too lazy to get divorced—is the puppet master. "Al! You're gonna love Al! You look just like his wife, the one who died of cancer. The poor thing, she really suffered," she says. But Al doesn't seem to notice or care that I bear even a passing resemblance to his deceased bride or any other living thing for that matter. He can barely tear himself away from his phone. I want to ask him if I can strap it to my forehead so we can at least pretend this is something resembling a date.

♥

Date #59: Stink

My second date with Emmet. We meet for dinner again, and it's pleasant enough, not good, not bad, *comme ci, come ca*, as he and the French would say. But who needs lukewarm? When dinner is done, we walk together to our cars. It's November and an unusually warm night. At my car, I thank him for the evening.

"You're welcome," Emmet says. "Do you mind if I smell your neck?"

"Whaaaa—?" my jaw drops, and before I can answer, he leans in and sniffs my neck behind my ear, taking a deep whiff.

"Ahhhh!" Emmet says, seemingly pleased.

WHAT THE HELL? I take a giant step backward and while keeping a wary eye, open the door to my car. He struts over to his own, an American-made convertible. "Your smell!" he calls after me. "Now I need to drive with the top down!"

You stink. I get in my car and lock the doors. The soft top of Emmet's convertible folds back like an accordion, and he waves and speeds off into the night.

Freak. Goddamn freaking freak.

When I get home, I delete my online dating profiles. I can't take this anymore.

♥

Someone has sent me a registered letter. My heart leaps up—could it be from Jack?

At the post office, the clerk has me sign for it. I take a deep breath and wonder if she sees my face is flushed. Back in my car, I study the white envelope addressed in slanted, loopy script, posted from Massachusetts. But this is from long-lost Zach, the moody, bearded younger man who dumped me, who I've not heard from in months. Who broke both my and Evie's hearts. Inside is a note:

> Holly,
> I just wanted to tell you one more thing . . .
> Thank you.
> —Z.

And he's returned my love letters to him, the Christmas, birthday, and anniversary cards. No, thank you. It's Zach who deserves the thanks. And I sit there in my car holding his letter, remembering his countless hours of listening and patience, over many months, as I talked about my divorce, crying, agonizing; some of my life's darkest hours made better by his unwavering support. How hard it was on him. How he loved me. I will always be grateful.

Zach has let go.

And then, a few days later, I receive a text from Jack:

> Got your thoughtful letter. Thank you. Will respond via the same medium J.

Every day now, I go to the mailbox and check for his letter, but the mailbox is always empty. Days pass and the letter never comes. Days become weeks, and I'm still going through the day with a heavy weight in my chest, still hoping, yet deep down understanding this is all likely futile, but still, I hope. Hope is a stubborn thing.

After nearly a month of torture, I decide this is silly. Just talk to him and understand if anything has changed because this is all so very hard on me. It's the lack of resolution that keeps me hanging.

I call Jack on a cold Sunday night because I know he's always home on Sunday evenings and, sure enough, he answers. "How are you?" I say, not knowing what I'll say next.

A big exhale, bordering on a groan. "Alright, I suppose. Just relaxing here in my recliner." I teased him about that chair; how he seemed permanently glued to it.

"They're going to find your body in that thing."

"What?"

"Wait—that came out wrong." *Geez, Holly*. Nervous laughter. "I was joking."

And after this ridiculously awkward start to the conversation where, for a second, Jack may have thought I was threatening to murder him, he apologizes for never having answered my letter.

"I started writing it," Jack says. "On my iPad."

"Oh. You didn't want to just email it, then?"

"No. Letters have to be handwritten," he says.

"Oh. Well, would you tell me what it says?"

He tells me that he cannot offer me more than what we had before. A casual relationship but nothing more than that, and he knows, too, that this is unacceptable to me.

And I tell him that I understand and I thank him for letting me know and I wish him well. And then I hang up.

Now I know. And I wonder how I've so loved someone who clearly doesn't love me in return and why I've clung to this one-sided attachment for so long. And I think about how Jack has changed my life and I wonder if I ever changed his in any way and then I have a really good, messy cry. Because none of that matters anymore. This is done. I need to let go.

And later, when I feel like I can't cry anymore, I call Rose, my voice hoarse and quiet. She will just listen to me croak out the last of my story with Jack. As we hang up, she says, "I'm going to send you a poem."

"Oh, let me guess . . ."

"No," Rose says, "It's not the 'if you love someone, set them free' bullshit."

"Oh God!" She's got me laughing again. "If it returns, it's yours, if it doesn't, it never was."

"No, if it doesn't, you hunt it down and kill it."

"In his recliner." I pause. "Oh my God, I can't believe I said that about the recliner!" Rose snorts as she laughs.

"It's by Stephen Dunn," Rose says. "You'll like it."

> *Lovers*
> To keep the one you want
> dig up a footprint of hers
> and put it in a flowerpot.
> Then plant a marigold, the flower
> that doesn't fade.
> And love her.

If she's distant now
it's for a reason beyond control.
So don't tamper with the impressions
left by her body when
for the last time she leaves your bed.
Just smooth them out
and forget her.
Who is not vulnerable
to a stronger magic (the
broken glass, the bullets
in a yawn),
the terrible power of the one
less in love.

God, yes. The terrible power.

Or perhaps worse: the terrible power of the one who never loved at all.

♥

Heartbreak and colds are both worse first thing in the morning and late at night. Today I've got both. Seems half the time there's a feeling of tears simmering right behind my eyes, or maybe it's my bad sinuses, but I'm pretty damn miserable. One foot in front of the other. I know, that in time, this should get better.

I take the train into the city for a lunchtime economics lecture at the Pierre Hotel in New York. It's a way for me to stay connected to my former life and colleagues.

The ballroom is packed with at least a hundred people, and it's a high-tech affair with all the latest audiovisual bells and whistles, headsets, a large screen, and slick visuals. The lights are dimmed and the director of equity research takes center stage to talk pharmaceuticals.

Midway through his talk, there's a banging of chairs, some urgent whispers at the table next to me. Two middle-aged men stand, holding an elderly man to his feet as he pitches forward, gagging. They bolster him as he shakes and heaves. I've had some first-aid training, and for a second, I wonder if the man is having a stroke or heart attack. "What's going on?" I whisper.

"We don't know. He was eating and then all of a sudden he starts making a noise . . ."

"Sir, can you speak?" I ask the man in distress. "Can you tell us what's happening?" He cannot. He shakes, his eyes flutter.

"I think this man is choking," I say. "Quick! Let's get him over here on the floor—on his side—and see if there's something in his throat."

With the heel of my hand, I whack his back behind his shoulder blades. Nothing. I take two fingers and sweep his airway and then he vomits on me. A good sign. He's breathing and seems better. We cover him with a jacket to keep him warm until the ambulance comes, and I hold his hand and tell him that everything is going to be okay.

When the paramedics take over, I slip out to the ladies' room to wash the vomit off my clothes, my heart still racing. Yet somehow, I feel better, I feel grateful. I've helped someone, and this moment has jolted me back to reality and put everything in perspective. Just being alive is what matters, and all this other nonsense is just that: nonsense. Hearts heal. Everything is going to be fine. I'm going to be fine.

I check my phone and find an email from David:

> Holly,
> I'm at an investment seminar at Yale today and happened to meet Alton Manley. He seems like a very nice guy.
> David

Are the planets colliding? What are the chances?

A nice email from David. And I call him right there from the ladies' room and we have the most hilariously awkward conversation where he tells me that he met Alton, who marched right up during lunch and introduced himself as having dated "your wife." I shriek, deny this is the case because we never dated, David laughs, I assure him we were never a serious item, and our conversation is a reconnection of sorts. David and I are bonding over Alton Manley of all people. We talk a minute about Evie and I tell him I'll call them after school.

This has been quite the day already. I return to the luncheon and take my seat.

♥

CHAPTER 26

Sun and Snow

Date #60: Don't Be Surprised

November, back in California for some sun while Evie is with David. I admit it, I'm still in a slump. I'm here in the hopes of snapping myself out of my mourning for Jack, thinking a break in the routine might help. I'm here to see Graham, too.

When I get into town, I head to a pizzeria for a quick bite. The hockey game is on, Boston Bruins playing Toronto. I know that, at this moment, somewhere in the country, Jack is watching, too. Toronto is winning and I want to rib him. But I don't. To have severed our regular contact has been far more painful than I ever imagined. "I could do with a friend," he'd said in Charleston and I'd scoffed at that. Now it's me who needs one more than ever.

There's the start of friendship with firefighter Graham. While our connection is vastly different than it was with Jack, Graham and I have grown closer. I admire his down-to-earth quality and common sense, how he gets out of bed every day happy about his life, content with his place in this world and makes it a little better. But I'm realistic. There's no future here, given our twelve-year age difference and living on separate coasts. Not to mention that we're at different places in our lives. He needs to get married, he needs to have his babies.

On my way home, I buy champagne because I remember Graham likes it, and when he walks through the door, I literally catch my breath, he's that striking, even just in jeans and a T-shirt.

It's been three months since we've seen each other and there's some foreignness at first, yet the trust remains. And it's beautiful to be together again, to feel the warmth and caring of another human being.

It's still early evening, and after a while, we wander out of bed. Graham says he wants to brush his teeth so I ask if he wants a toothbrush. He says he's already brought one. I see that he's got it there, the "cover" being some toilet paper wrapped around the bristles to keep it clean. I tease him and we laugh. I stand at the bathroom sink watching him brush for what seems a very long time. "Still brushing?"

"Yeah, my dentist told me to brush for two minutes," he says.

"You're not going to have any enamel left! You are the original Boy Scout."

We go to the kitchen and turn on the TV and watch basketball and eat chips and salsa. He's horrified when I say "Who's that?" as they interview a player.

"That's LeBron James! How do you not know who that is?"

I shrug. "I like basketball, I used to play. But there's not many mature women's' basketball leagues in Connecticut," I say, laughing at the thought.

"Or black people," he says.

"Yeah. Not exactly diverse."

"How would your friends react if they knew you were seeing a black man?" Graham asks, looking at me intently.

"Well, some do know and they think it's great. And the rest that don't, wouldn't care either way. And if they did, I could not care less."

"Have you ever dated a black man before?"

"No. Who do you typically go for?"

"I've always liked playing in the snow," Graham says.

"What—you mean—"

"I've always liked white women."

We talk about Graham's future. He says that he feels that he "should" get married but doesn't necessarily want to. And he thinks he wants kids but sometimes isn't sure.

"Are there other African Americans at the fire department?" I ask.

"One other."

"Do you feel like you're treated fairly?"

Graham looks away for a minute. "Yeah," he nods. "For the most part. Though I've been on some calls where the general public have been difficult."

"Meaning . . .?"

"One guy who I was giving medical assistance to called me the 'N' word."

"What?"

"That's happened a few times."

"That is just beyond horrible."

"You're surprised?" Graham says.

"I am."

Now Graham looks surprised, looking back at me. "You shouldn't be."

"I'm just so sorry that as you put your own life on the line—"

"Why are you apologizing? It's not you," Graham says.

"Still . . ." I'm sickened at the thought of him being treated this way.

We finish watching the game, head back to bed, and curl up together, falling into peaceful sleep till morning.

♥

Back in Black's. Standing in the very spot where I met Graham, staring toward the room where Jack and I had that drink the first night we met.

I'm bored, I'm lonely, but I'm out. My plan for dating these days is to just live my life, get out the door, and try not to be a recluse. But no more online dating for now. I'm completely emotionally spent.

The band is on break and the joint mostly dead. I pick up a food magazine that someone has stashed in a corner and start reading. There's an article about kale.

"Are you really reading in here?" a young guy says to me. He's good-looking, with black, wavy hair and olive skin.

"Yeah. What's worse—I'm reading about kale."

"This is a bar," he says deadpan. No smile.

"Yeah, I know. I'm a nerd."

"You live in town?" he asks.

"No, but I'm here a lot. You?"

"Minneapolis. My name is Xander."

"Hi, Xander."

"How old are you?" Xander asks.

I almost spit out my wine and start to laugh. This guy's game needs work. "Does it matter? How old are you?"

"Thirty-one," Xander says.

"And I am forty-five," I say proudly, standing a little taller, awaiting his reaction.

"You look good," he says, sounding surprised.

Later, he'll tell me that I have "beautiful collar bones" and will admit to cheating on his girlfriend. How did she find out? "She got a hold of my phone," he says.

I ask if they are still together. "No. She broke up with me."

"Oh, that's hard. I'm sorry," I say kindly. "Tough lesson to learn."

"Are you a mom?" Xander says. "Don't act like a mom in a bar. You're supposed to be sexy."

"Wow." This guy is unbelievable. Apparently, kindness is distasteful and birthing a baby makes you revulsive?

It's moments like this when dating feels extra hard, extra burdensome. When I want to yell "Can women ever win?" Be sexy, but not too sexy, otherwise you might be branded a slut. And don't be motherly or too kind, either, because that's not sexy. And don't be yourself, either, pretend to be something you're not. Walk the tightrope, woman. This isn't about you.

♥

Date #61: Thankful

Thanksgiving Day, late at night. Graham has driven for four hours after Thanksgiving dinner at his mother's to visit me.

There's a sweetness and familiarity. He leaves, and when I awake alone in the morning, it's as though everything was a dream.

Having Graham in my life is something to be thankful for. While we may not have a long-term future, my life is better right now with him in it. And in the brief time we've known each other, he's opened my eyes to things I've needed to understand. What it's like to be a black man in America, for starters.

♥

CHAPTER 27

Rule Breaking

Date #62: Just to be Loved

Neil is the son of professors, born and raised in Nebraska. I had to break two *Rules* in order to meet him.

Eating dinner alone one night at a restaurant, I noticed the man sitting next to me. Thick gray hair, baby face in a pinstripe suit, nervously glancing over his shoulder, like he was being trailed by the FBI. Every thirty seconds, he shoulder-checked, with curious facial expressions, ranging from fear, alarm, despair, to boredom, intensely scanning the crowd. After a good ten minutes, I finally said, "Is everything alright?" (First violation. Don't ever speak to a man first.)

Neil held up his phone, revealing an open dating app, and I laughed. "A first date?" and Neil and I began talking. Conversation flowed easily, he explaining he's a management consultant, based in Washington, DC, but is often in New York and Boston.

From the crowd, a petite woman with long brown hair appeared. "Neil?" she said shyly.

"Ashley?" Neil said. His date had arrived.

Ashley said she needed to go to the ladies' room but she'd be right back. As Neil paid his tab, I slipped him a piece of paper. "Here's my email address if you'd like to get in touch." (Second broken rule. Let the man ask for your information.)

Two hours later, Neil emailed, saying he wished he'd had dinner with me instead of Ashley.

Now Neil and I are finally out at an Italian restaurant in Midtown. It's close to Christmas, and New York City is chilly and festive with lights and decorations, all the bars and restaurants packed with holiday revelers.

We enjoy dinner together shoulder-to-shoulder at the bar and laugh and talk easily. He says his date with Ashley wasn't the worst one he'd been on.

"Tell me about the one that was," I say.

Neil had a date with a woman who got so drunk, she spewed racial epithets in a bar, and when Neil whisked her out of there, she insisted on stopping by his nearby apartment to use his bathroom. She emerged completely naked, chasing him through his apartment, crying, "I just want to be loved! I just want to be loved!"

Maybe I'm not doing so bad at dating, after all.

After dinner, Neil hails me a cab. "I'll see you in the new year, I hope?" he says.

"I'd love that. I had a great time."

"Merry Christmas," he says, kissing my cheek.

♥

Date #63: Six Things

California. The week between Christmas and New Year's. Graham comes over for a late-night evening visit and we stay up talking a long time. I ask him more about what it's like being a minority in a predominantly white community. "Does it help that you're a firefighter?" I ask.

"Sure. If I get pulled over by the cops for speeding or something, I take out my ID showing I'm a firefighter. It's the first thing I do."

"Smart."

"There are six things that every black man knows," Graham says.

"What's that?"

"Avoid getting pulled over for small infractions like a broken tail light by keeping your car up-to-date. If you're pulled over, keep both hands in the air or on the steering wheel. Try to stay calm and be overly respectful. Look straight ahead. Loudly say what you're doing and explain every movement. Do not reach for anything, and if asked, make sure you verbalize what you're doing as you reach."

"Geez—how do you know this?" I'm stunned by how quickly he's rattled off the list.

"It's a code of conduct that's been developed," Graham says.

"I've obviously been clueless about the extent to which this is a different country for African American men."

"Racial tensions have been high for a long time. It's starting to surface now," Graham says. "At least technology is starting to expose the corruption." He gets up and walks to the chair where he's folded his clothes. I lie in bed and watch him dress in the candlelight, thinking about everything he's just said, feeling the weight of it in a way I've never before. Caring even more now because now I care for him. Graham comes over and bends down to give me a kiss. "Night," he says.

"Drive safely. Text me when you get home."

"I will," he says over his shoulder, quietly closing the door behind him.

♥

Date #64: James & Maddie

It's the left coast for New Year's Eve, and I'm watching a couple on the dance floor. The way they look at each other, it's unmistakable: they're in love.

I've forced myself out of the house tonight, vowing to start this new year right. No moping or self-pity allowed.

The song ends, and the adorable lovebirds wander over, say hello, order some champagne. "I have an extra one," the woman says, handing me a glittery silver party hat.

"Oh thank you," I say, laughing, and the three of us begin talking. They're James and Maddie. She's well into her champagne and keeps blowing her party horn and giggling. James shakes his head at her and grins. She's a neurosurgeon from Dallas, he's a screenwriter in L.A.

They tell me they've been in a long-distance relationship for four years, that they've had many ups and downs, but they're serious about each other. A couple years ago, one night during a bad patch, they stood outside in the back alley behind Maddie's apartment and had an all-out screaming match. They broke up. They got back together. Maddie explains she's a devout Christian and was a virgin until she was thirty-seven years old. James was her first. "Look!" he says. "Her ears aren't even pierced."

We three talk and laugh until the clock strikes midnight, and as we toast a new year and happiness and their relationship, I make them promise to keep me posted on how they're doing. And they make me promise that I'll stay strong and not settle and that I'll wait for the right man, a good man. Meeting these two, I'm reminded of the way love looks: the way James looks at Maddie.

A few months later, an ecstatic Maddie will text me a photo of a diamond ring, exclaiming that she and James are engaged.

♥

Date #65: Survivor

I'm at The Starling, eating at the communal table.

Seated next to me is a good-looking guy having dinner with a group of friends. Preppy looking, thick brown hair, blue eyes, tall. He introduces himself and says his name is Parker. He tells me he's local and a pilot, that he and his father survived a plane crash in the Atlantic, off the coast of Maine two years ago. On his phone, he shows me a video, shot by search and rescue from a helicopter, hovering over choppy seas, as first his father, then Parker, are hoisted to safety by stretcher, just as their plane sinks. "I didn't even get wet!" Parker says.

Later that night, he sends me a text:

> It was really great meeting you. I think you're beautiful. Looking forward to hearing from you.

I tell Parker that I'll be back in California in a few weeks and let's stay in touch.

♥

CHAPTER 28

Real American Stuff

It's the second week in a brand-new year. I'm back in New York and have dinner at the bar at Gramercy Tavern.

A married couple out celebrating their fifteenth wedding anniversary is chatting with me. "A good day in marriage is a day without homicide," the wife says.

A text comes in from Parker the pilot. We talk about weekend plans and he says, "Sunday might be fun to fly up to the high desert, land on a dry lakebed, and shoot some guns. Real American stuff. I'd love to do that with you sometime."

I text Luke about Parker's idea of a good time:

> **Luke**: What woman wouldn't want to be flown to a remote place with an armed man?
>
> **Me**: Right?
>
> **Luke**: Is he going to throw in leather "bracelets"?
>
> **Me**: Ha!
>
> **Luke**: Dry lakebed? Don't get on an airplane with a dude with guns.
>
> **Me**: Chill, baby, I'm back in New York now.
>
> **Luke**: We should save time and just issue the Missing Persons Report now.

♥

Date #66: Girl, Dig My Vibe

Rod struck up a conversation with me one night in New York while I was waiting for friends to join me for dinner. He was eating a massive pork chop slathered in gravy and asked if I wanted to go out sometime. I liked his taste in food, at least, and he seemed interesting enough, so I said sure.

We meet on the Lower East Side for a drink on a cold January night in a cozy, hard-to-find bar in a back alley.

We get to talking, and Rod tells me his business: industrial lubricants. Lube!

Luke has a field day:

Luke: As in Big Dick's Oil & Lube?

Me: No. Industrial lubricants. Big machines and such.

Luke: For the hardest, largest jobs?

Me: Exactly.

Rod is a smart dresser. He likes bespoke clothes, but only ones made in the United States. Not Italy. Specifically dislikes Italian cuts. And while Rod's business is lube, he's really a musician.

"Do you play an instrument?"

"No," Rod says. "But I sing."

"Anything I might've heard?"

"No, but I once gave a cassette tape to Pat Benatar's manager."

"Cassette tape?"

"Yeah! Remember those?" he says.

"I do. Pat Benatar, too." I bite the inside of my cheek so I don't start laughing.

Rod leans in and looks at me more closely.

"What?" I say.

"How come you don't have more wrinkles? At your age? You do something to yourself like those girls?" he says, studying my face, squinting.

"Like those *girls*?" I say, squinting back. "So how you come you never married? You're almost fifty?"

Rod nods. "I was serious a few years back about a girlfriend who got ovarian cancer and had her ovaries removed."

"Oh, sorry."

"I broke up with her because she couldn't have kids. I really liked her." He grimaces. "I'd even stopped doing all that James Bond shit and really started opening up."

"James Bond shit . . . I know exactly what you mean." I finish my drink and tell him I need to get home.

Next day, he'll ask me out again and I'll politely decline. "If you don't dig my vibe then, okay, but I think you are one sexy girl," he texts.

Girl. Who should have more wrinkles.

♥

Date #67: Margaritas & Mole

The I-Just-Want-To-Be-Loved Date from Hell Survivor is back in town. This is nice Neil from before Christmas, who disappeared for awhile. Rose is staying with me for a few days, and when Neil asks me out, I agree, provided Rose and I can cook him dinner at my house.

When he arrives, we've got the Latin music playing and the tequila begins to flow. Housemade margarita mix and Rose's *mole* simmers on the stove. "Our chaperone knows her way around a kitchen!" I joke.

"It's called a threesome now," Neil says.

Over dinner, Rose tells Neil that she and her boyfriend of three years have recently split. They'd been talking of getting married.

"We need to get you back out there, girl," I say.

Rose buries her face in her hands. "I'm not ready," she says.

"You don't go into this thinking you're going to find the love of your life. You're just having fun, meeting people," Neil says.

After dinner and many margaritas later, Rose excuses herself and goes upstairs to bed.

It's after midnight now, and Neil moves closer to me on the sofa. *What are you up to?* He touches a lock of my hair, gently twirling it around his finger. We sit like this for a while, quietly talking as he plays with my hair. I find it very sweet, it's such a simple and intimate thing. And then as we say look at the time and talk of him having an early start at the office tomorrow, he leans in and kisses me good night.

And I don't feel much. I don't feel much of anything, sadly. No chemistry. Damn it, oh damn it, because this is a really great guy.

But it will all turn out fine. Because Neil is right; this is about meeting new people and making new friends. Neil and I remain friendly to this day.

♥

Date #68: Anchorman

By mid-January, I finally have the energy to give online dating another shot, but this time it needs to be different. I'm going to try Tinder, an app that's all about swiping right or left, yay or nay, based upon an initial impression of a photo. Instead of miniscule photos, long narratives, and emailing, Tinder has sizable pictures and gets you straight to conversation via texting. Brock, my first Tinder date, is a TV anchorman who looks like Buzz Lightyear. "I'm an Ironman, too," he says proudly.

"An Ironman anchorman!" I say, trying to keep a straight face.

"That's right," he says. He's handsome in a classically American football jock kind of way. It's obvious that Brock, who I really want to just call Buzz, takes good care of himself, even going so far as to dye his hair. It's a brassy shade of blonde, and I can see a touch of gray roots peeking through. Hair dye is to broadcasting like hardhats to construction.

Buzz says he last dated a former Ford model. "What happened to her?" I ask.

"She said we don't have a spiritual connection," he says, putting "spiritual" in air quotes.

"Oh."

"I'm a writer, too," Buzz says after I tell him what I do. He pulls out his phone to show me his blog: *What's Wrong with You?* is the title. Brock is frequently asked that question, he says. Fifty years old and never married—people just don't understand.

A photograph of his former fiancée, a blonde anchorwoman in Texas, is posted on his blog as evidence that he's not entirely hopeless.

Indeed, there isn't anything noticeably wrong with Buzz, as far as I can tell. Sure, he's a little vain, but he's sincere, smart enough, seems he'd be a devoted boyfriend. But there's . . . there's just something missing. Is it spiritual? Maybe that's it.

♥

CHAPTER 29

Going Hungry

Date #69: Four-Legged Third Wheel

Back in sunny California to escape East Coast snow. Parker the gun-toting pilot asks me to dinner, and we meet at a Japanese restaurant near his apartment. He tells me that he's thirty-nine years old, has never married but hopes to someday. He wants kids, too, like his sister, who lives nearby. I tell him about Evie. "I love kids. I wish I'd had more," I say. I remain silent on my age and he doesn't ask. I don't say aloud that having more children is out of the question for me now, being nearly forty-six, and I wonder if Parker has asked me out because he thinks I'm younger than I actually am.

Over sake and sushi, Parker tells me he's lived most of his life in California, with the exception of the time that he fell madly in love with a German girl he met in college. He lived in Germany with her for a while and they nearly married. Parker talks of his love of flying, and his father. That on his sixteenth birthday, Dad put his gift in the driveway: a brand-new red Porsche that he'd drive to high school every day. He's a trust fund kid who helps his father with the family businesses in aviation and real estate. He's an accomplished sailor, too.

Parker asks me about my childhood and I tell him the truth: it wasn't easy. Not easy at all, and then Parker tells me about his father's difficult childhood, how his dad is completely self-made. How his father was given away, too, pretty much an orphan. "You remind me of my dad," Parker says, and I think about the fact that it's something that no man has ever said to me before. After dinner, Parker says, "Would you like to meet my dog?"

"Your dog?" Is this some kind of euphemism?

"I've got a Springer Spaniel. Dexter." We walk around the corner to Parker's apartment to meet Dexter, who takes a shine to me. The dog is young, only a year old, long-haired, with a reddish-brown and white coat.

While Parker fixes me a drink in the kitchen, Dexter cozies in next to me on the sofa, resting his head in my lap while furiously wagging his tail.

"Oh, he really likes you!" Parker calls.

"He's adorable!" I say as Dexter licks my hand.

Parker sets my drink down on the coffee table. Dexter growls. "Dexter!" Parker warns, giving the dog a fierce look. Parker sits down next to me and Dexter barks. "Don't be jealous," Parker says sternly.

Parker inches closer to me and Dexter puts his paw on my hand. I start to giggle. Parker takes my other hand in his and now I'm really laughing. "I've never had a date quite like this before," I say, stuck in the middle, squeezing Dexter's paw and Parker's hand.

Parker turns to kiss me and Dexter begins barking loudly. I pull away because I'm laughing too hard.

Parker and I make plans to have dinner again later in the week.

♥

Date #70: Hunger

The next day, Graham comes over. "How come you're in town?" Graham says, standing in my kitchen.

"Better weather, I guess."

"You went out last night?" he asks with a half smile, as though he might know something.

I look at him, then glance away, a little guiltily. "Yeah, a date. How about you?"

"Saw a movie . . ."

"A movie, huh. Alone?"

"Nope," Graham says coyly. "With someone. We're not exclusive," he quickly adds. "So, what do you think of this guy?"

"You know, it's early days, but I like him . . ." Graham comes over and puts his arms around me. I pull back to look him in the eyes. "She's your girlfriend?"

"Not a girlfriend," Graham says, firmly. "She's young, a preschool teacher."

"Blonde, I presume . . ."

"Yep."

"Do you think she might be someone you could be serious about?"

"I don't think so . . . I had someone I really liked, but she moved to Portland. Do we have to keep talking right now?"

I laugh. "Too much talking, huh?"

Later, we laze in bed and I ask him again about his mother, his sister. "We're both putting in overtime to help Mom out," he says. And Graham will tell me again how hard his mother struggled to raise him and his sister, how she worked hard to raise them right. "There was no question I was going to college. She wouldn't take no for an answer. Made sure I got a scholarship."

"She sounds like a force."

"She is. My college tuition was all covered, but my meals weren't included. Sometimes I went hungry."

"I've been on my own since I was sixteen," I say. "I had some of those times, too."

"My coach knew," Graham says. "I'd open my locker and find paper bags that he'd stashed in there. Sandwiches and stuff."

"Sounds like a great guy."

Graham agrees. "And he never let me thank him or even talk about it. We both knew we weren't going to talk about it."

"You know, there are some really good people in this world," I say.

"Yep."

"You're one of them." Graham pulls me closer and kisses my forehead.

♥

Date #71: Somewhere in the Seventies

Parker takes me to his yacht club for dinner. It's a warm night and we sit outside on the patio, drinking wine, eating steak and lobster, watching a pink and amber sun sink into the Pacific. A seagull lands near our table, staring longingly at our bread basket. Parker bats it away with the flick of his hand, making a face. "Reminds me of when I was a kid," he says. "We were bad sometimes. One of my friends had been given a shotgun for his birthday. We were about thirteen or fourteen and went down to the nature preserve near the beach . . ." Parker points behind us. "And in about five minutes, we shot probably fifteen seagulls out of the sky."

"You didn't . . ."

"And we knew we were in trouble and had to hide the bodies, so we throw them in a bag, we take them home to my friend's house, and when his mom sees them, she freaks out because it's against the law. Especially in a nature preserve."

"So then what?"

"His mom told us to start plucking the birds and we did, and it's feathers everywhere, and then she deboned them, saving the meat."

"Seagull meat?"

Parker grins and takes a big gulp of his chardonnay. "Yep. And his mom wraps up the meat real nice and takes it to the local homeless shelter."

"She did not."

Parker nods. "She did. Told them it was goose."

"And they ate it?"

"I assume they did, yes," Parker says, laughing.

"Wow." I stare back at Parker, and instantly I think of Graham going hungry, the sandwiches left in his locker.

Parker drives me home and I ask if he wants to come in for a drink. I open a bottle of wine, pour two glasses, and we sit next to each other at my kitchen counter. "Tell me about this book you're writing," he says. "What's it about?"

"Well . . ." I pause. We clink glasses. "It's about dating, about what you do when your life doesn't turn out as you'd planned. About divorce in middle age."

"Okay. Middle age?" Parker looks at me. "Do you mind if I ask how old you are?"

"I'm forty-five."

Surprise, disappointment, flash across Parker's face in a split second, and then he quickly recovers, masking his feelings with a pleasant smile. "Wow," he says. "I thought you were younger than me."

"Thirties? No . . ."

Parker sets his glass down on the granite countertop a little too hard, almost hard enough to break it. "So, it's a book about dating?"

I begin to feel a little uneasy. "Yes. It asks whether you can find one really great boyfriend in a hundred dates."

"A hundred dates?"

"And by the way—it's hundred *dates*. I'm not sleeping with one hundred guys! God." I shake my head, pouring a little more wine into his glass and a lot more into mine. "I decided to go on one hundred dates, well, hopefully less, and to just write about the experience." Parker's eyes widen in apparent horror. I squeeze his arm. "No, listen, I'm changing names, ensuring privacy."

Parker locks eyes with me. "And I'm date number *what?*"

I swallow hard. "Um . . ." I pause to think. "In the seventies, I think."

"I'm date number what?" Parker says, his voice cracking, slumping over the counter, burying his face in his hands. For a second, I'm afraid he might be crying, but then he turns to face me and his anger is unmistakable. "And I really liked you," he says.

"It's not like that. I like you, too. I'm dating, just like you do, right? The only difference is that I'm writing about it."

Parker glares at me. "I need to go."

I grab his arm, but he wrenches it away. "Listen, I'm really sorry. I never intended—"

Parker is already out the door. I watch his car speed out of the driveway, and this time it's me slumped at the counter, burying my face in my hands. I feel like a monster. I start to cry. Have I taken this too far?

♥

Date #72: Not Just a Number

It's been a terrible day. From the moment I woke up I've felt sick, sick about everything, sick about Parker, questioning everything. I'm an idiot. I'm an idiot that I think I can find love, I'm an idiot to even admit to this ridiculous quest, but I wasn't going to lie to Parker. By mid-afternoon, I've dragged myself out the door for a walk at the beach when my phone rings. It's him, and I tell him I've been a mess. "Are you more upset about my age or that I'm writing a book?" I ask.

"It's not your age."

"Have you ever dated an older woman?"

"Well . . ." He pauses. "Not dated," he says, and then we both laugh.

"It's not my intention to hurt you or anyone, but I wanted to be honest about my book, because you asked. You're not just a number. But I know now, too, that I'm not what you're looking for. You can't have babies with me."

"I don't care. I love that you're different, interesting."

"You said you want a family . . ."

"You've lived your life. You remind me of my dad, you remind me of myself."

Two hours later, Parker is at my door with a bouquet of sunflowers.

He tells me that he wants love, to be happy, he tells me again that I'm like his dad. "I always get the girl I want," he adds.

"Parker . . ." I shake my head. "I feel like you don't know the real me. That you just like the idea of me. When your parents were buying you that Porsche to drive to high school, my mother had already given me away. Our lives have been so different."

"You are a lady," he says.

I find a vase and fill it with water. Parker watches me cut the stems of the sunflowers. "Thank you for these," I say, arranging the flowers. He tells me that his mother belongs to a garden club. That I'd like the garden club, that I'd like her and her friends. "When are you back in California?" he asks.

"In a couple of weeks."

"Can we get together again?" Parker asks.

"Sure," I say. "I think we should talk some more."

♥

CHAPTER 30

Much to Sing About

Date #73: Frigid February

Ugly Uggs with treads sturdy enough for a monster truck—a Connecticut winter must-have. I throw on jeans, a silk camisole, and a cardigan, and trudge off into the snow for my first date with a guy who lives in my town. My expectations are low.

Kurt, whom I've met on Tinder, is Swedish American and has chosen a neighborhood oyster house just a few blocks from my house to have a nightcap. The frigid weather has scared off other patrons, and I'm the only one there, seated at the brick-walled bar. The bartender, arms folded across his chest watching TV, looks over and smiles half-heartedly.

There's a blast of cold air, and in walks Kurt, his cheeks flushed pink, his hair a dark shade of red. A ginger. He's adorable.

Kurt rips off a gray wool glove and shakes my hand, smiling, a smile that lights up the room. He settles in beside me and we start talking and don't stop. We just click. Like me, he has only one child, a daughter, around Evie's age. Like me, he grew up in the Pacific Northwest and moved to the East Coast after living abroad. He loves the outdoors. He's a professionally trained opera singer, and for fifteen years, he lived and traveled the world, performing.

"That sounds amazing. I know very little about opera," I admit.

"I didn't either. Until college. In high school, I was into football. Played quarterback."

Beneath his sweater, I can see his athletic build, his broad chest. If anything, the football seems more natural than the singing. He's an all-American kind of guy, yet sophisticated. He tells a story of when he was performing in Rome and was running late for his show and his Roman taxi driver treated this like a true crisis, driving over sidewalks and stunt driving to get him to the opera house on time.

We keep talking with another round of drinks until the bartender clears his throat and we get the hint that it's time to leave.

Outside my house, Kurt gives me a tiny peck good night.

And after he's left, and I text him my thanks for the drinks and an enjoyable evening, and Kurt answers that "We have much to sing about."

And I absolutely believe that we do.

♥

Date #74: Mixed Skills

Anyone who can persuade hard-living rock stars to check into Betty Ford has got skills. Tyler was once the manager of a famous heavy metal band and, after that, a TV executive for fifteen years. He's good-looking with a thick head of gorgeous brown hair, an infectious grin, emotionally available, very smart. He knows a lot about just about everything. He's a single dad of two who seems to really love his kids. He lights up when he talks about them.

But when it comes to skills with the ladies, he moves a little too fast for my taste. We meet for margaritas at a Mexican place, and within half an hour, he just grabs my face in his two hands and plants a big, open-mouthed kiss on me. I recoil. It's too much, too soon, I tell him. I'm uncomfortable now, and I compare that discomfort with the incredible ease that I felt the other night with Kurt. But I do like Tyler, and when he asks if I'd go out with him again, I agree. But I put him off. I'm very busy, I say. It will have to be after I return from California.

♥

Date #75: Duets & Cough Drops

It's a night for comfort food and jammies. And hot tea with lemon and honey and a giant box of Kleenex. I've got a cold. When Kurt calls and asks me out to dinner, I tell him I hope he doesn't mind if I'm sick and a little drippy. "Not at all. You poor thing," he says.

Kurt picks me up, and when I get in the car, he hands me a bag. "What's this?"

"Some things for your cold." Inside I find cough drops and Kleenex, vitamin C, and an assortment of cold medicines.

"That's so thoughtful," I say, staring at him in amazement. "Thank you. I'd give you a kiss but I don't want you to get you sick," I say, patting his arm.

We go to an Italian restaurant softly lit by candlelight, and the maître d' leads us to the best table in the house, directly in front of a roaring fire. Kurt wears a cashmere sweater, a tweed sport coat, and jeans. He's a sharp dresser. In the fire's reflection, his eyes are like large pools of blue water, open and kind, tiny crinkles at the edges when he smiles—and he is always smiling.

We drink red wine, order pasta, eat off each others' plates, laugh and flirt. We talk of our girls, how they both love music. Kurt's daughter, Hannah, like him, is a singer.

He drives me home. In the driveway, Kurt gives me three little kisses good night on my cheek. My heart pounds. We sit there in the car a moment, just staring at each other. "Can I come in for a tour?" he asks.

"A tour? Okay," I say, and he cuts the engine.

I turn the key in the lock and open the door, flick the lights. Nothing happens. "That's odd," I say. "None of the lights are working." I fumble in the dark to find another switch. Still nothing.

"Maybe a blown fuse?" Kurt says. "Where's your box?"

"My box?" I start to giggle, and then Kurt and I bump noses in the dark.

"Your *fuse* box," Kurt says, laughing. By the light of his cell phone, we make our way to the basement, and within minutes he's fixed the problem. All lights on, all systems go.

As I'm fixing us drinks, I hear a few notes of music. Kurt has found Evie's electric guitar in the living room. "I didn't know you played guitar," I call to him.

"A little."

I sit opposite Kurt and he begins to sing, "I know a girl, who says that she loves me . . ." and I listen as he sings a love song I've never heard before that he'll later tell me is "Jill" by Harry Connick Jr. Kurt locks eyes with me, and I get chills hearing this powerful voice, rich and warm, like nothing I've heard before. This man is talented.

"Your voice," I say, shaking my head. "Wow."

As he carries the last note, I clap and Kurt beams. "Thanks. What's one we can sing together?" he says, looking off thoughtfully a minute. He begins to strum the first chords of U2's "All I Want Is You."

"Yes! I love that song."

And together Kurt and I sing in duet, shyly smiling, looking into each other's eyes:

> *All the promises we break*
> *From the cradle to the grave*
> *When all I want is you*
>
> *All I want is you*
> *All I want is you . . .*

Kurt sets down the guitar and says, "I want to come over there and give you a proper kiss. Like really kiss you," he says. "But I'm a little afraid."

"Afraid?"

"Only your cold. I've got a performance next week and I'm going to need my voice."

"You don't need my cold, that's for sure. What are you performing?"

"Puccini, 'A Time for Us' in Italian, 'Phantom of the Opera,' 'Time to Say Goodbye.'"

"That's amazing. I wish I could see you. But I'm in California next week."

Kurt lingers a little longer, he on one side of the room, I on the other.

At the door, when he leaves, we embrace. "Let's get together again before you go to California," he says.

"Absolutely."

♥

Date #76: Ironing Bored

Another one bearing scant resemblance to his picture. Do these guys use stunt doubles with hair for their online photos? Preston is bald except for a small patch of short, downy blonde hair in the middle of his head. Pink head, pink face, pink shirt, British accent.

"So, you work in consumer products?" I ask, trying to get the conversation rolling.

Preston nods. "Correct."

I'm imagining Procter & Gamble, toothpaste, deodorant, and such. "What kind of consumer products?"

"Ironing boards."

"Ironing boards?"

"I design ironing boards."

"I can say, without hesitation, I've never met an ironing board designer before," I say. "How do you build a better ironing board?" Preston beams. Then, for the next hour of my life that I will never get back, I'll hear more about ironing board design than any human could ever want or need to know. He takes out his phone and shows me his exclusive designs. Bright, cheerful little numbers, legs balanced on pontoons, like water bugs.

At the end of the date, he promises to send me a board.

The next day, I politely decline his invitation for a second date.

My board has yet to arrive.

♥

Date #77: A Proper Courtship

Last minute, Sunday night, Kurt asks if I have plans for dinner. I don't. "There's a really good Greek restaurant in town. I'll pick you up."

I'm still sick so we keep our distance. We sit opposite one another in the restaurant's white leather booth and order practically everything on the menu, not understanding that every portion is enormous. Dish after dish comes, and still we eat until we're absolutely stuffed. We laugh hysterically over the menu's repeated references to "personal cheese" and speculate on what that could mean.

"My mom is going to love you. She said to me 'Just find a nice girl,'" Kurt says, looking at me pointedly.

I remember very clearly the last time a man said that to me, but this time it feels different. "I can't wait to meet her," I say.

After dinner, Kurt comes in for a drink and sits on the opposite side of the room playing Evie's guitar and we sing again. Tonight, it's a lot of Elton John, whom we both love. We do "Your Song," "Candle in the Wind," and "Tiny Dancer" in falsetto, laughing like fools.

"This is like a proper, old-fashioned courtship," I joke.

"No, this is torture!" Kurt says.

We haven't even held hands yet, and even though we've only been on three dates, we just know. This feels right.

♥

Date #78: Toi-toi

My fourth date with Kurt, and because I've still got a hacking cough, our eighteenth-century-style courtship continues. "I need to see you before you leave for California," he says.

From opposite sides of my living room, Kurt and I talk about everything that has brought us to this point in our lives. He's been divorced for nine years. Eight months ago, he separated from a girlfriend he'd been with four years. He tells me that he nearly died two years ago from diverticulitis. He lifts his shirt to reveal a scar on his abdomen.

I tell him about my tumor and I pull back my blouse to show him the scar that snakes from my shoulder blade to my ribs.

"I've been looking for you," I tell Kurt.

"And I for you," he answers.

As he leaves, I tell him that I hope his performance goes perfectly. "What do you say for luck? 'Break a leg'?"

Kurt shakes his head. "You say 'toi-toi.'"

"Toi-toi, Kurt."

He opens the door and says, "I'm going to tell my parents about you."

♥

CHAPTER 31

Roses and Cashmere

As I fly west, I know that in a short time, everything has changed. I will need to have some conversations when I reach California.

♥

Date #79: No Celebration

Graham comes over, and the minute he sees my face, he knows something is up. "Everything okay?" he asks. I shrug and pour him a glass of wine. No champagne this time. This isn't a celebration.

"I've met someone," I just blurt out.

Graham looks down at the floor and nods. "Okay . . ."

"We can't see each other anymore. It just wouldn't be right."

"I understand."

In the coming days, Graham and I will talk several times more by phone. We'll talk about what we shared and how wonderful it was to have our time together. We'll talk about love and how it's unmistakable and how sometimes you take what you can and sometimes you hold out for everything. Our conversations will lead Graham to decide to find his one that got away. The woman in Portland.

"I hope you find your happiness," Graham says.

A lump forms in my throat. "You too. I will miss you."

♥

Today is Valentine's Day, and ironically, now that I've finally met someone I'd actually like to spend the day with, he's back in Connecticut and I'm in California. My doorbell rings and it's a floral delivery. Two dozen long-stemmed red roses from Kurt and a note:

> Holly, my gorgeous muse,
>
> Happy Valentine's Day!!!
>
> You're the sweetest, most sexy, beautiful, and playful person, inside and out.
>
> Thank you for coming into my life. I look forward to knowing you more and

more each day and experiencing, together, all the wonderful things that life has in store for us.

Love,

Kurt xoxo

♥

Date #80: Roses, Roses

Late afternoon on Valentine's Day, Parker asks by text if he can come by to bring me something. "Okay," I agree, with dread. I take the vase of roses from Kurt and the note and hide them in the laundry room.

Soon Parker arrives at the door, handing me a bouquet of long-stemmed red roses. "Happy Valentine's Day," he says, kissing my cheek. He's smartly dressed, in a collared shirt beneath a sweater and dress pants. I thank him, my heart sinking. I offer him something to drink, and then we sit together on the sofa. The smell of his cologne wafts through the room. He smiles at me, expectantly. "You look great," he says.

"Thanks. So do you. You're so tanned."

"Yeah, I've been doing a lot of sailing," Parker says, nodding.

"Since I saw you last, a lot has happened."

"What number date are you on?" Parker asks with a grin.

"Too high to count. Just kidding. I think you should know that in all seriousness, I've met someone really wonderful."

Parker's face clouds. "You mean since you were last here?"

"Yeah. And . . . I know this sounds ridiculous, but this feels like the real thing."

Parker clears his throat. "You're the only girl I'm bringing flowers to today, you know," he says, crossing his arms, and then he laughs, high and shrill. "I've got a lot of stalkers, as I call them, who just hang outside my apartment across the street waiting for me, who were hoping for some flowers."

"I'm really flattered. I'm sorry."

Parker will try to kiss me, Parker will try to do more than kiss me, and I will tell him no. He will leave angrily again, and this time it will be for good.

♥

Date #81: Let Me Take Care of You

When my flight lands in New York, Kurt says to text him once I'm home in Connecticut. He wants to bring me dinner.

In the car home, I try not to think too hard about this leap of faith I've taken. Kurt and I haven't even held hands and yet. My cold is gone, his show was a success, there's nothing holding us back now. What if the physical isn't there?

"Sit down," he says in my kitchen.

"No, no, let me get you a drink, you're at my house—" I protest.

"You're tired. You've been on a plane all day. Please, let me take care of you." I sit down at the table and melt into the chair. I am tired. Kurt brings me a glass of wine and then kneels at my feet.

"What are you doing?"

He holds up a pair of orange socks. "Cashmere," he says, slipping them on my cold feet, and I'm speechless.

There are also two dozen roses, a hot roast chicken with mashed potatoes and Brussels sprouts, and chocolates for dessert.

We find our way to bed. Our instincts were right. So right.

♥

Date #82: Without Trying

Kurt and I see each other as much as we can. One night, after Evie is asleep, Kurt comes over, I run a bubble bath, and we get in the tub together and talk as we drink wine. He says, "Something that feels completely right without trying is perfection and meant to be."

I lean forward through the bubbles and kiss him. "You're right," I say.

"You make me want to do things I've never done with anyone before."

"I feel the same way." And Kurt and I talk about introducing our girls to each other and of he and I taking a trip together somewhere in the coming weeks.

The next night, Kurt comes by the house to meet Evie. We are in the kitchen, and Evie is practicing her violin when she sees Kurt pass by the front window. She runs to the front door and throws it open. "It's you," she says.

♥

Date #83: Sledding with the Girls

Overnight, there's been a massive snowfall and school is canceled. Kurt calls and asks what Evie and I are up today. "Just keeping warm here by the fire," I answer.

"How'd you like to come sledding with Hannah and me?"

"You mean have the girls meet?"

"Yes." A warm feeling rushes through me. We have already discussed what this might mean. That he, like me, doesn't introduce his daughter to just anyone.

Evie and I drive over to Kurt and Hannah's house less than a mile away from ours. All this time, he was less than a mile away. Hannah opens the door and smiles shyly. With long, dark, straight hair and brown eyes, she looks nothing like her father except that they share the same radiant smile. "Do you like hot chocolate? And chocolate chip cookies?" I ask and Hannah answers that she does.

"We brought marshmallows, too," Evie says.

The four of us pile into Kurt's car and spend the afternoon sledding at a nearby park. Kurt brings his camera and takes pictures of the kids laughing and hollering as they fly down the hill. He takes pictures of me, too, with Hannah and Evie, of me in a spectacular wipeout, all limbs, upside down, backward in snowbank, capturing all the fun of the day.

Later, the four of us are back at Kurt's house, and over hot chocolate and cookies, he catches my eye. Our eyes meet and we both know that this day couldn't have gone any better.

♥

Date #84: Vegas, Baby

Las Vegas. I've never been, but I'm here now with Kurt, where we've come for a quick, romantic getaway. We've got a convertible, a great hotel, and some unexpected company, too.

Last week Kurt called his parents and told them that we were taking our first vacation together in Vegas. "That's funny," Kurt's mother said, "we're there next week, too. We have to get together!"

And this is how I come to meet Kurt's lovely parents, Barb and Ron, at a buffet dinner in the basement of their hotel, along with his aunt and uncle, who are all in from Portland. They could not be warmer or more welcoming. After everyone returns from the buffet, we tuck in to our dinners and I glance around the table. Everyone is brunette. "So, where does Kurt's red hair come from?" I ask.

"I've been asking Barb that question for years," Ron says and we all laugh.

"My side, I think," Barb says. "I'm Swedish."

Then the six of us are off together to a Bobby Vinton concert. I'm shocked to learn the man is still alive. "I had the biggest crush on him when I was a girl," Barb says.

Bobby comes on stage and sings his classics, and the six of us sing together, along with him, songs like "Blue Velvet," "Mr. Lonely," "I Love How You Love Me." Kurt's voice carries, so loud and distinct that it catches the ear of Bobby Vinton's daughter, who's performing onstage alongside her father. After the show, she pulls us from the audience and whisks us backstage. And that will be my first photo with Kurt's family, backstage with Bobby Vinton, snapped just at the moment as Bobby tickles me in the ribs.

♥

Date #85: Singing with EJ

Kurt surprises me with tickets to an Elton John concert at Caesars Palace. Just the two of us. We can't stop smiling or holding hands or singing. We sing our hearts out, we sing until we're hoarse. Some of the very first songs we ever sang together, back at my house: "Don't Let the Sun Go Down on Me." "Tiny Dancer." "Can You Feel the Love Tonight?"

♥

Date #86: Just Like That

It's our last day in Vegas and friends of Kurt's host a barbeque at their house. Kurt's mom and dad are there, his aunt and uncle too, along with still more of Kurt's friends from the time when they all sang together at the same opera house, and children and dogs, a cacophony of laughter, spontaneous *a capella* singing while more and more food just keeps coming off the grill. As the day comes to an end, when it's time to leave, Kurt's parents want photos. "I need a new picture of you both to frame for the living room," Kurt's mom says, smiling, smooshing me together with her son and snapping photos.

Later, when Kurt is off talking with his dad, Kurt's mom comes over and hugs me. "We think you're wonderful," she says.

Driving back to the hotel, top down in the convertible, Kurt looks over at me and grins.

"What?" I say. He looks guilty.

"I'm still kinda hungry."

"Me too! How is that even possible? We've been eating all day!"

Kurt whips the convertible off the freeway to an In-N-Out Burger drive-through. We sit outside in the convertible as the sun sets over the desert, stuffing our faces with burgers and fries. Kurt looks at me and laughs. "You've got ketchup all over your chin," he says, nicking it off with a finger and eating it. "I love you," he says. Just like that, so easily, so casually.

"I love you, too," I say.

♥

CHAPTER 32

Around the Table

Back in Connecticut after Las Vegas and I just feel off. Hard to put my finger on it. Low energy, sloth-like. We did burn it at both ends, eating, drinking, not getting a ton of sleep. I pull out my calendar. When was my last period? I count. I'm just a few days late. It's probably a nasty case of the lovely premenstrual syndrome. I turn the page on the calendar and see that it's nearly April, too, and soon, my forty-sixth birthday. Kurt keeps asking how I want to celebrate.

Throughout the day as I unpack from the trip and pay bills and grocery shop, I cannot shake the feeling that something is wrong. I'm just dragging and feeling cranky. What's particularly odd is that my breasts are sore. That hasn't happened since I was pregnant with Evie. What a paranoid, ridiculous thought. I'm far too old, and I've never, ever, been accidentally pregnant. Never, ever.

By late afternoon, I've had it, because my instinct is telling me something is wrong. I need to take this ludicrous worry off the table. I get back in the car and drive to the outskirts of town to a pharmacy. I don't want to bump into anyone I know seeing me buy a pregnancy test. Why? Because that would just make me look insane.

At the drugstore, I buy two different brands, both promising results just days after a missed period. *I am crazy.*

Just do the test.

In the bathroom, I follow the instructions on the box. I haven't peed on a stick in a decade, since before I had my daughter. Why? Because I'm ancient. I can't be pregnant.

Get this dumb worry out of the way. Then I can return to being the sore-boobed, bloated, someone-just-harpoon me, premenstrual bitch that I am. My sweats and Granny panties await.

Don't watch. I put the test on the bathroom counter and head downstairs to the kitchen and set the timer on my phone. Five minutes. You could unload the dishwasher, you know.

Or not. My friend Google soothes me with the statistic that the odds of getting pregnant at my age—exactly two weeks shy of my forty-sixth birthday—are about 2 to 3 percent, just slightly higher than the failure rate of the pill. Nearly impossible. So there.

I unload the top rack and then the alarm sounds. I dash back upstairs, my heart pounding. The test is crystal clear: PREGNANT.

This can't be happening.

For the next few minutes, I pace around the house, not going anywhere in particular, wandering aimlessly.

What do I do? What do I do? I'm pregnant?

Finally, I snap out of my trance and pick up the phone. I call Rose. "Are you okay?" she asks.

"No. No, I am not. I'm pregnant!"

"What?"

I am trying not to shriek. "I just did a test. And it says I'm pregnant."

"Oh my God!" And then Rose starts laughing. Long, hard, deep, hysterical laughter.

"ROSE, THIS ISN'T FUNNY!"

She's still laughing. "I'm sorry. It's just so funny. Do you know whose it is?"

"What do you mean? Of course I know whose it is! It's Kurt's."

"Was wondering about the fireman."

"Shut up."

"What are you going to do?" she says.

"I have no idea! I was hoping you could help me figure that out." I'm back to pacing again. Thank God Evie isn't witnessing this.

"Have you told Kurt?" Rose asks.

"No. You're the first person I called."

"Okay. Are you going to tell him?"

"Yes." I'm trying to remember what Kurt is doing tonight. He's having dinner with Hannah. He should be free after that.

"Holly, it's going to be okay," Rose says. "I love you." And we promise to talk tomorrow.

♥

Date #87: On the Rocks

Kurt is standing in my living room. "How was dinner with Hannah?" I ask, my voice tight.

"It was great. We went for pizza. She says hi." Kurt comes over and pulls me close, kissing the top of my head. "Is everything alright?"

"Well . . ." I turn away and walk toward the bar. "Why don't you sit down? Can I get you a drink?" I call over my shoulder.

"Sure. Scotch on the rocks," he says.

I turn around and walk back in the room. "Kurt, I'm pregnant."

"Better make that a double."

♥

First thing in the morning I see my internist. "What's going on?" she says, breezing in with a smile.

I stare at her like a bird that's flown into a window. "I'm pregnant," I say and then the tears that I've been holding back begin to spill.

By the afternoon, she's got me booked with an obstetrician.

♥

Date #88: Circles

Kurt sits with me in the waiting room, holding my hand. Silently, we watch a steady stream of pregnant women waddle in and out of the office. The door opens and next comes a woman cradling her newborn. She tells the receptionist that she's here for her one-week postpartum checkup. The nurses and office staff stop what they're doing and come over to admire the wriggling, pink baby. All of this seems surreal to me, that it cannot actually be happening. It's been a decade since a scene like this has been my reality.

The ultrasound technician moves the wand across my belly and the obstetrician peers at the screen. "You're very, very early," she says. "But definitely pregnant," she says, smiling.

On the monitor, all I can see are two circles. There's one large, which I know is my uterus, and within it, a tiny one at the bottom. I'm relieved that it's all there is. Nothing distinguishable, nothing babyish or beating, just a circle within a circle. "You can get dressed," the doctor says kindly. "We can talk in my office."

Kurt and I clasp hands again. "Do you know what you'd like to do?" the doctor asks. Kurt and I look at each other. Neither one of us speaks.

"We don't know," I say, finally.

"Okay," the doctor nods. "Let's talk through our options. If you decide that you'd like to try to do this, we can. I know of plenty of older parents, like you, who've gone on to have healthy babies. There are many tests we can do along the way to ensure the fetus is healthy and you stay healthy, too, Holly. Now, it's very early days. At your age, there's also a high rate of miscarriage."

"Which is?" I ask.

"Over 50 percent. As I said, we can just wait, and there's no reason to make a decision just yet, because it's so early. But if you're leaning toward a termination, then I recommend we do it sooner, rather than later. It's better for you," she says. "Physically and psychologically."

"We need a few days to think about this," Kurt says. "I mean, we just found out yesterday."

"Of course. Totally understandable," the doctor says. "I do think, though, that what we might do, just as a backup plan, is make an appointment at the hospital for next week for surgery, just in case. Just to have it on the calendar if that's what you decide to do." She turns to her computer and clicks through her calendar. "I have an opening on Monday morning," she says.

"We can change our minds if we need to?" Kurt says.

"Absolutely. Right up until the last minute," the doctor says.

"Let's do that. Let's hold that time, just in case," I say.

Today is Tuesday. We have six days to make our decision.

♥

Date #89: Torn

Kurt and I sit on the sofa together, side by side, staring straight ahead. "I keep seeing a little one toddling around the corner," he says. Kurt takes a sip of his scotch, the ice twinkling in the crystal glass. I'm not drinking. Should I be drinking? I want to be drinking. I don't even know what I'm doing anymore.

"I don't know what to do. I thought I couldn't have kids anymore. But I always wanted a second child," I say.

"I always wanted a son," Kurt says.

"I'm torn. So torn."

"Me too."

I turn to look at him. "I've even been having crazy thoughts that we should try having this baby just for Hannah and Evie. So that they'd finally have a sibling. A child that would bind us all together."

Kurt puts an arm around me. "Sweetheart, that's not crazy at all."

"And there's us. How long have we even known each other?"

Kurt picks up his phone and scrolls through the calendar. "About seven weeks, or so," he says.

"Well, I've already met your parents. I mean, what were we waiting for? It's time for a baby!" Kurt and I laugh a little. Weakly. This is one hell of a situation. And we have more conversations just like this, going around and around, undecided. Monday looms.

This is my last chance. My last chance to have another child, my last chance to have the baby of the man that I love.

♥

Date #90: A Dearest Friend

It's Friday. I'm quickly being reminded by how early pregnancy sucks. I remember this now, this feeling like hell. Within the last day, I've developed a backache and have lost my appetite. Continually nauseous, and I have to go around pretending everything is normal, especially in front of Evie. She cannot know this is happening. But I have something to look forward to: dinner in the city tonight with Luke. My Luke, I need him, my buddy, my brother. I need to just sit with him, one of my oldest friends, and talk. Talk this through, even without Kurt, even as much as I love Kurt. Because Luke will always have my back. Because I know that, in the end, this is my decision to make. If I choose to have this child, it'll be my life that changes the most profoundly.

On the train into Grand Central, I stare through the dusty, gray window and see that it's starting to rain. Everything looks bleak. I think about how hard I've worked to build this new life for me and Evie, and now this. Is this pregnancy an unexpected blessing, a second chance at a lost dream, or will this threaten everything?

Luke and I meet up at a restaurant on the Upper West Side near his apartment. He knows my predicament. When he sees me, he smiles a little sadly and gives me an extra long hug. "You're glowing," Luke says.

"So, so, not funny," I say, laughing. This is exactly what I need. To laugh.

We order dinner but I'm not even hungry. Luke gets a glass of wine. "Not drinking?" Luke says. I shake my head.

"I just don't know," I say.

"You do know, Holly," Luke says, meeting my eyes. "What do you know?"

I stare down at the table. "I know there was a time, for a very long time, that I wanted this baby, I wanted a second child. So badly . . ." Luke reaches across the table and squeezes my hand.

"Continue," he says.

I'm crying now. "This baby is from a time in my life that no longer exists, a time that is gone. This baby is not part of the new life I've intended for Evie and me."

"That's right," Luke says. "And on Monday, as hard as it is, you need to go to that hospital."

"I know, I know. And I've been thinking, too, that so much of the misery of my childhood was set in motion by my mother's accidental pregnancy. I can't let history repeat itself."

Our food arrives and I can barely touch it. My nausea is worsening, and now I'm feeling cramping. It reminds me of the miscarriage I had before Evie.

"You okay?" Luke asks.

I shake my head. "Really don't feel well. Maybe it's just the emotional upset? I'm sorry I'm bad company tonight."

"Oh babes, please!"

Luke and I walk toward his apartment. "Come up for some tea or something," Luke says.

I nod. My cramps are getting worse.

Riding in the elevator up to Luke's apartment, I nearly double over in pain. "What's happening?" Luke says, helping me into the apartment.

"I need to go to the bathroom," I say.

I sit down on the toilet and see my underwear. There is blood. And now, a lot more blood. My body has taken over.

♥

Date #91: Scents and Sounds of Home

Tonight, for the first time in several days, I feel like myself again. I have a great burst of energy and head to the grocery store, buying chicken, potatoes, apples, and blueberries. I cook my grandmother's recipe for chicken paprikash and make mashed potatoes and apple-blueberry crisp with vanilla ice cream for dessert. The day has been overcast and damp, so I light a fire to cut the cold, and then I hear the front door open and slam shut.

"Hi, honey!" a voice calls. It's Kurt. He and Hannah come into the kitchen. The smell of cinnamon and baking apples fill the house, and soon there's the sound of Hannah and Evie chasing each other, laughing, blasting music, wrestling on the floor like rambunctious pups.

Kurt sits at the counter and talks with me quietly as I cook, telling me about his day, and I tell him about mine before we call for the girls to start their homework. Evie and Hannah thunder in, stacks of papers, books, and computers in hand, settling in side by side in front of the fire to do their work.

Later that night around the table, I pause to appreciate each person that I share this meal with, and I'm reminded of how some of life's simplest things can bring the deepest pleasures. A meal, a shared communion, companionship. I reach out and take Kurt's hand and he looks at me. He looks at me with love. Kurt, Hannah, Evie, and me. We four. There is love at this table.

♥

CHAPTER 33

Spring

Pink cherry blossoms bobble in the breeze outside Evie's school. The seasons have changed again, and tonight is her spring concert. Evie will dance, sing in the choir, and play her violin. She's gone ahead to have dinner with David before the show.

I run through the parking lot, sneaking in a side door of the auditorium half a minute before curtain, the lights beginning to dim. I scan the rows for an open seat, but the place is packed with parents, grandparents, siblings. There's two people waving at me. I climb the stairs in the dark, and as I grow closer, I am surprised to see that it's David and his girlfriend, Adrienne. "Hi there," Adrienne whispers.

"We saved you a seat," David says, patting the chair next to him.

"Thank you," I say, a little stunned. This hasn't happened before. I sit down next to David, the curtain falls back, and there is Evie standing with her choir on the riser in her new blue dress, a ribbon tied in her hair. Her eyes search the audience and when she sees us, she breaks into a smile and waves. We wave back. She beams and the music begins.

The voices of young children rise up, filling the space, filling my heart, their voices pure and true. I think about everything that has brought me, brought us, to this moment. I marvel at that astounding girl on stage, I think of the man sitting next to me and how, without him, I wouldn't have the most beautiful thing in my life. Our Evie. And I'm profoundly grateful for everything that's come before in this life because it's made me who I am. I'm grateful for what I have, which is so much, and for what's ahead. For all of us.

♥

About the Author

Holly Martyn was born in Toronto and raised near Vancouver, Canada. When she was eighteen years old she bought a one-way ticket to Tel Aviv and set off on a solo journey to the Middle East and Europe until finding her way to New York City where she became a successful Wall Street executive.

Holly is a graduate of Columbia University and has studied writing at the University of Iowa's Writers' Workshop, Oxford University, University of Cambridge, and holds a Master of Fine Arts degree in creative writing from Queens University of Charlotte, North Carolina. She lives with her daughter and dog in Connecticut and California.

Acknowledgments

I began writing more than a dozen years ago and many have helped me on my journey to my first book.

Ashley Warlick, with thanks for your editorial expertise and for believing from the earliest days. "This is your book, Hol," you said.

Iowa Writers' Workshop and Chris Offutt for your mentorship and encouraging me to dedicate myself to writing.

Pinckney Benedict, deepest gratitude for your expert guidance and friendship.

My thanks to Jamie Widdoes for early lessons on artistic vulnerability and your enduring support.

Great appreciation for my teachers and editors, Adrienne Brodeur, Lauren Groff, Michael Kobre, Fred Leebron, James McKean, Susie Mee, Naeem Murr, John Murray, Jenny Offill, Jem Poster, Steve Rinehart, Elissa Schappell, and Olive Senior.

Thank you to my readers Natasha Freestone, Karenmary Penn and Chris Shirley for your time and patience in making this a better book.

I'm also indebted to Anita Absey, Jane Bohan, Cody Brown, Chris Ceccotti, Carla Damron, Terry Dreyfus, Steve Eoannou, Nikki Finke, Amanda Groves, Melissa Groves, Sara Whalen Hess, Dartinia Hull, Beth Johnson, Mary Kaczmarek, Mitchell Kriegman, Josh Lebowitz, Dr. Ze'ev Levin, Vanessa Livingston, Kathryn Manning, Phil Marino, Alice Martell, Vittoria Natarelli, Barry Perlman, Sonia Prashar, Eric Sherman, Chris Shirley, Ashleigh Taylor, John Temple, Natali Tofiloski, Gitte Toft-Nielsen, Charles Tolbert, Barb Ward, Ron Ward and Kathy Webber.

A special thank you to my publisher, Marta Hallett, for enabling me to publish the book that's true to my original intention.

And finally, my love and thanks to my daughter and her father, who were among my earliest cheerleaders.